for 1000+ tutorials ... use our
free site .... drawinghowtodraw.com

Copyright © Rachel A. Goldstein, DrawingHowToDraw.com, 2018

All rights reserved. No part of this book may be reproduced or transmitted in any form or by any means whatsoever without express written permission from the author, except in the case of brief quotations embodied in critical articles and reviews. Please refer all pertinent questions to the publisher. All rights reserved. No part of this book may be reproduced or transmitted in any form or by any means, electronic or mechanical, including photocopying, recording, or by an information storage and retrieval system - except by a reviewer who may quote brief passages in a review to be printed in a magazine or newspaper - without permission in writing from the publisher.

BY RACHEL GOLDSTEIN

DRAWING CHIBI SUPERCUTE CHARACTERS 2
EASY FOR BEGINNERS & KIDS (MANGA / ANIME)
LEARN HOW TO DRAW CUTE CHIBIS IN ONESIES AND COSTUMES WITH THEIR SUPERCUTE KAWAII ANIMAL FRIENDS

CUTE MAGICIAN

1. Draw an oval. The dotted line shouldn't be drawn. It is just a guide line.

2. Draw an "M"-like shape for bangs and 2 curved lines.

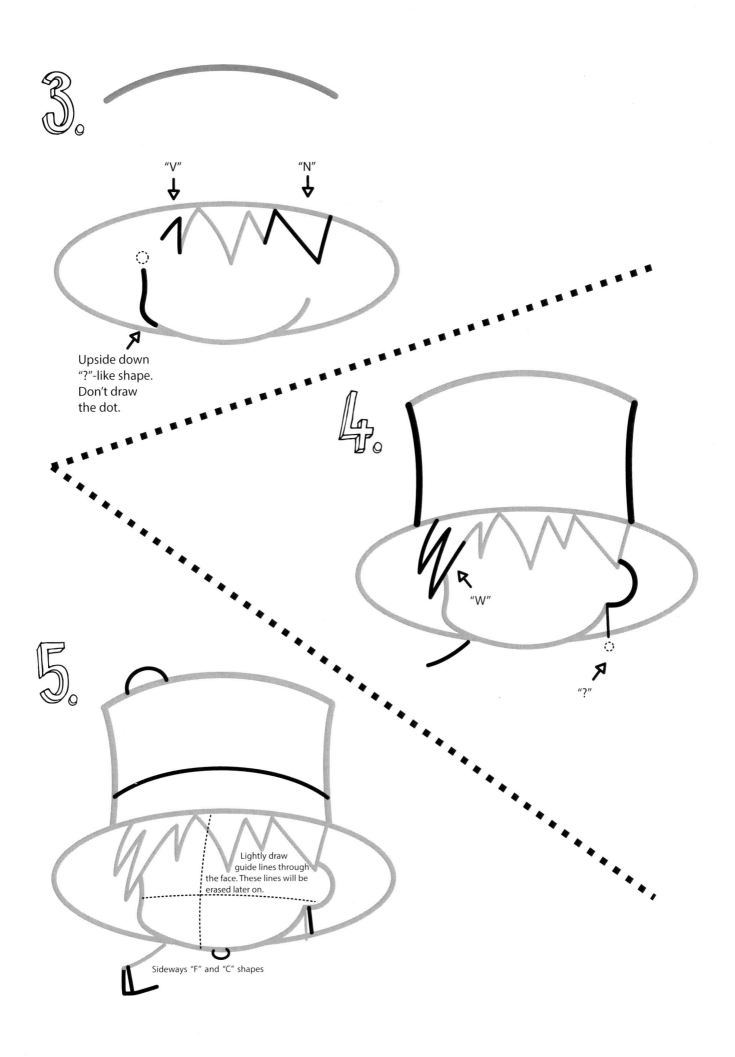

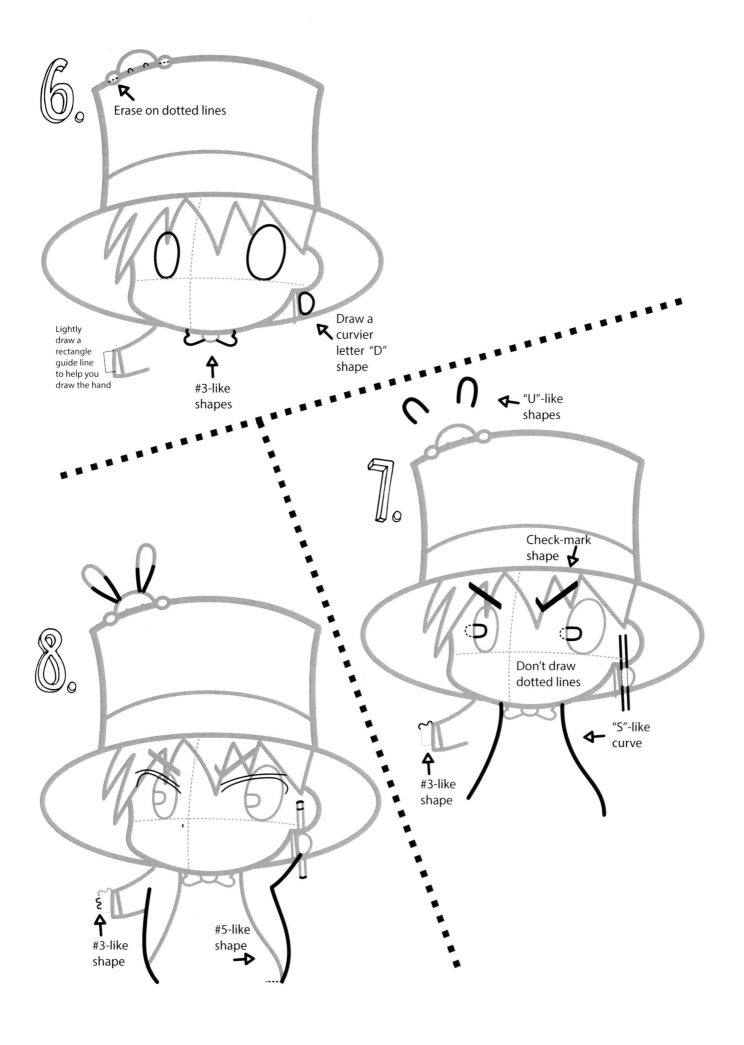

CUTE SEALS

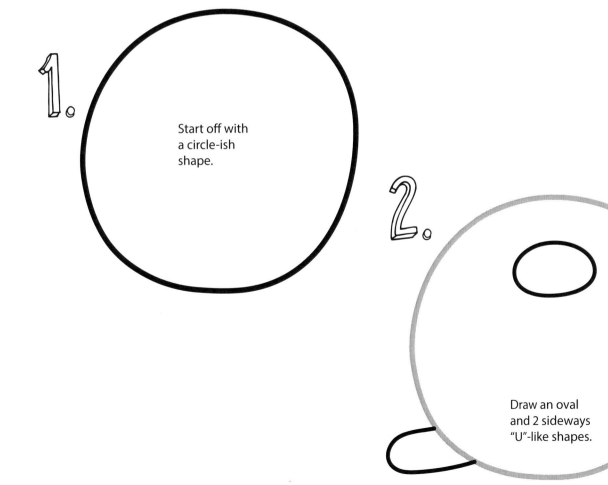

1. Start off with a circle-ish shape.

2. Draw an oval and 2 sideways "U"-like shapes.

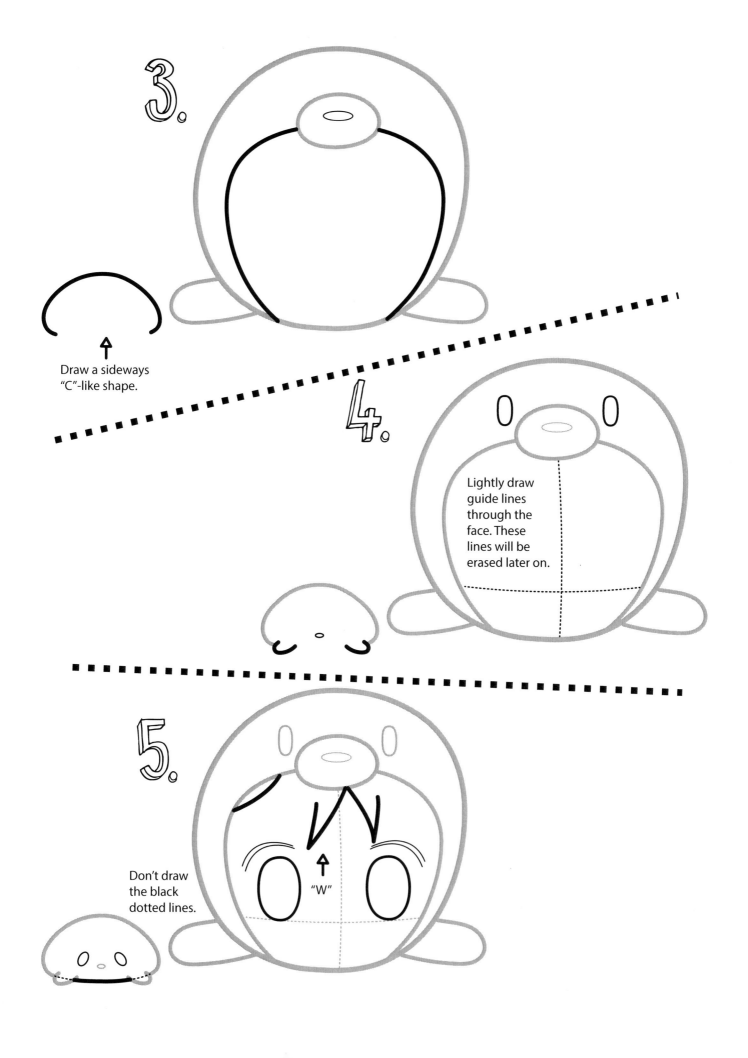

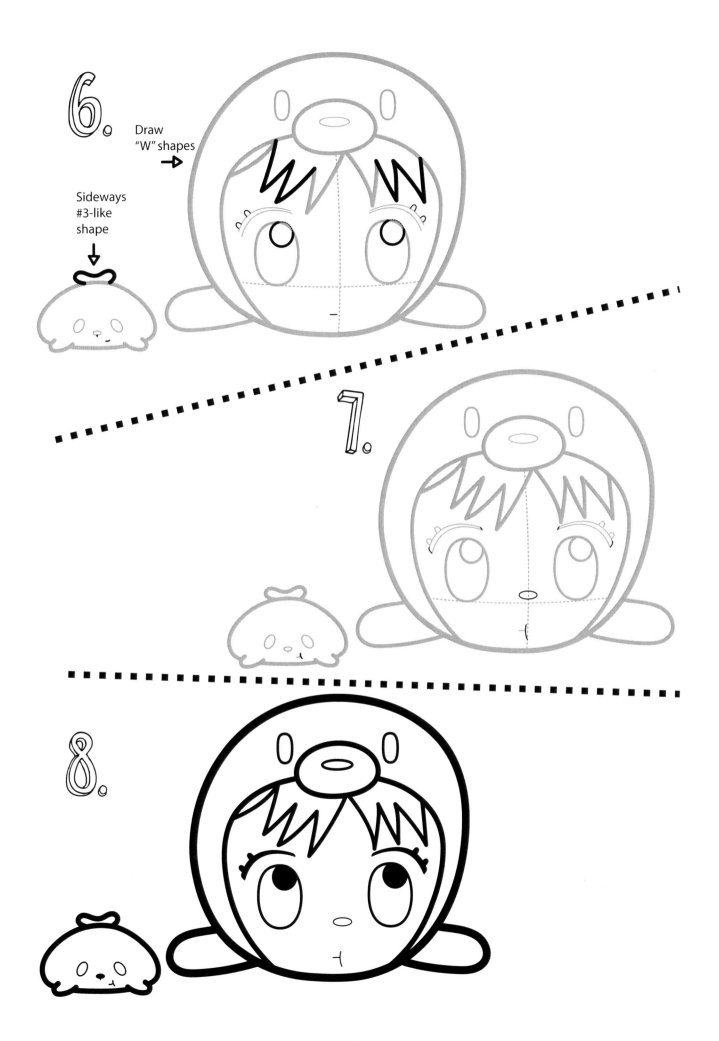

CUTE LITTLE WITCH

1. Draw a flattened oval. Lightly draw the dotted line. Part of this area will be erased later on.

2.

Letter "W"-like Shape

Lightly draw the dotted guide lines. These lines will be erased later on.

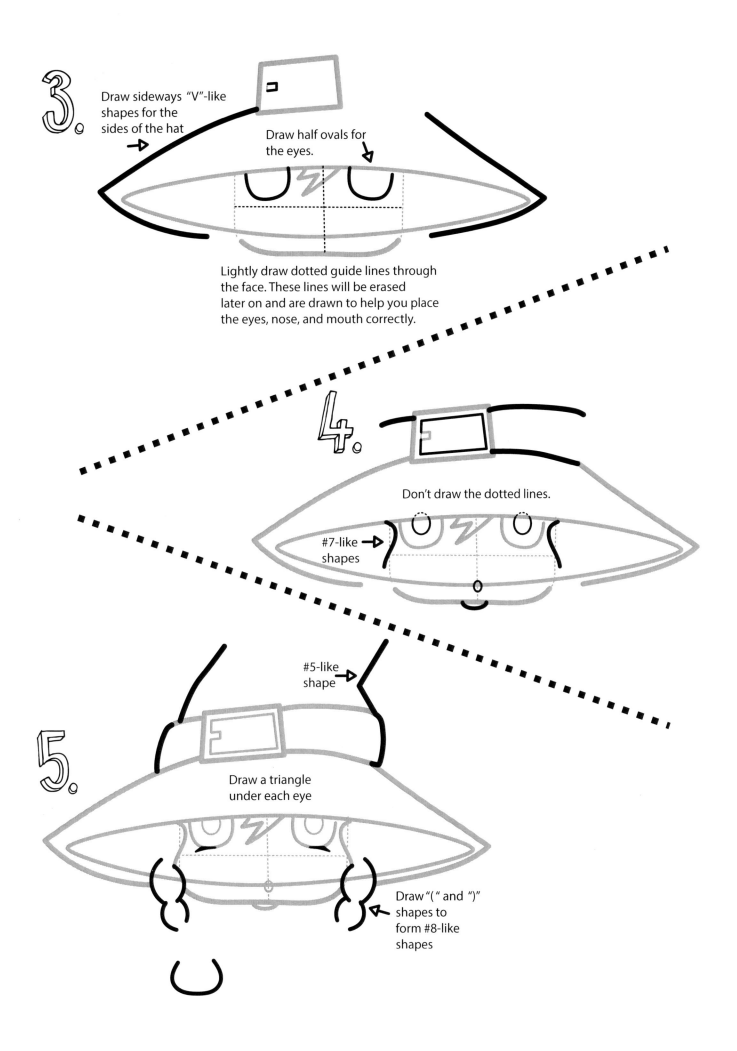

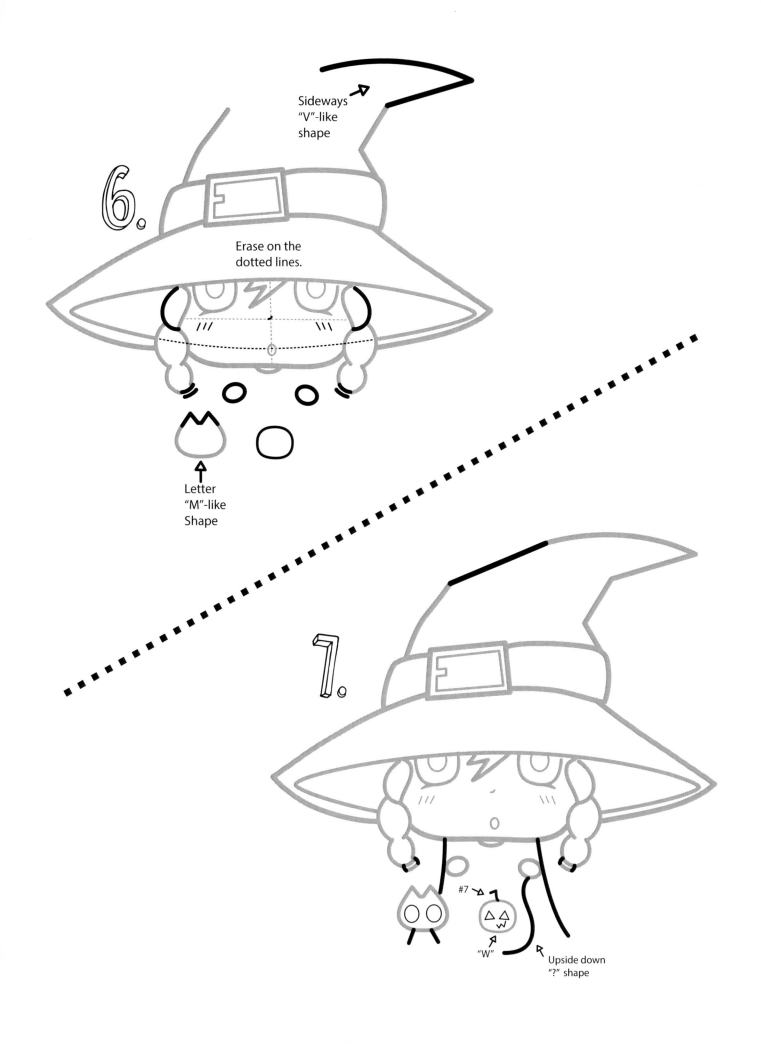

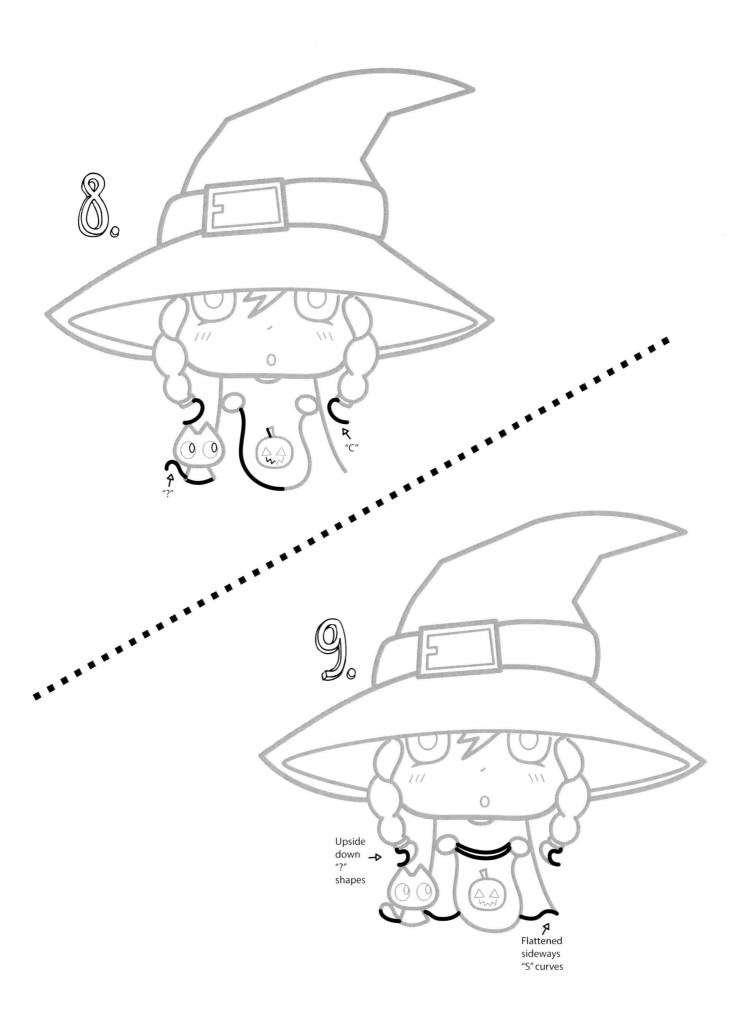

CUTE PUSSY CATS

1. Draw a line that curves around, almost like an oval. This doesn't have to look exactly like mine (It's just the outside of the hood).

2. Letter "V"-like shapes for ears.

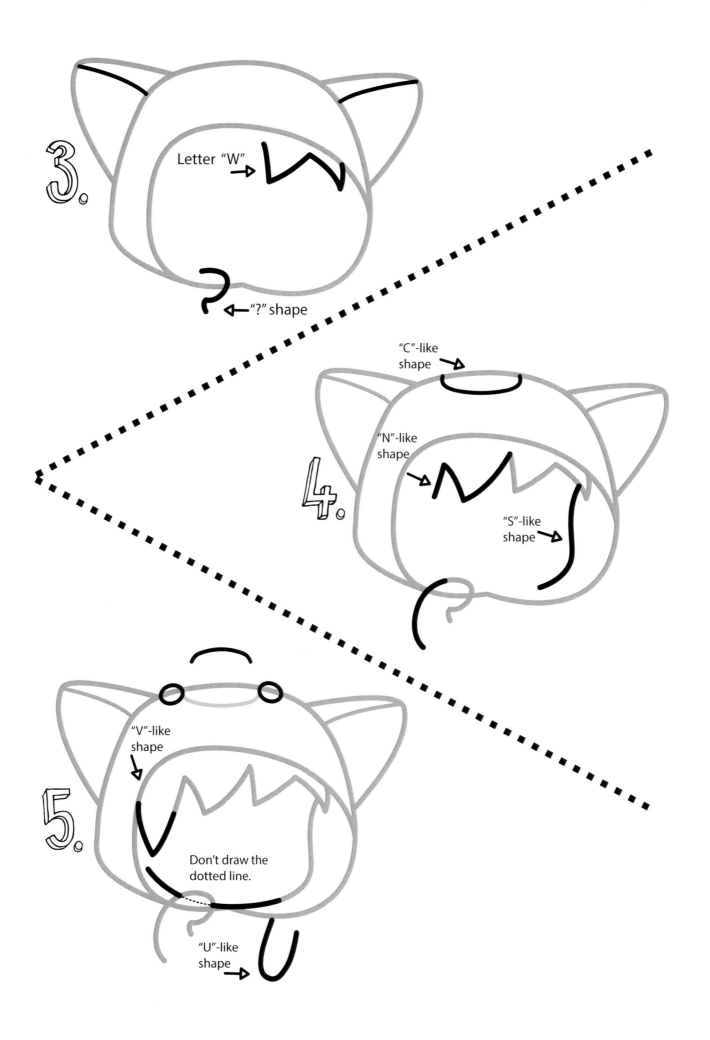

CUTE CHEFS

1. Draw a sideways #3

2. Backwards "C"

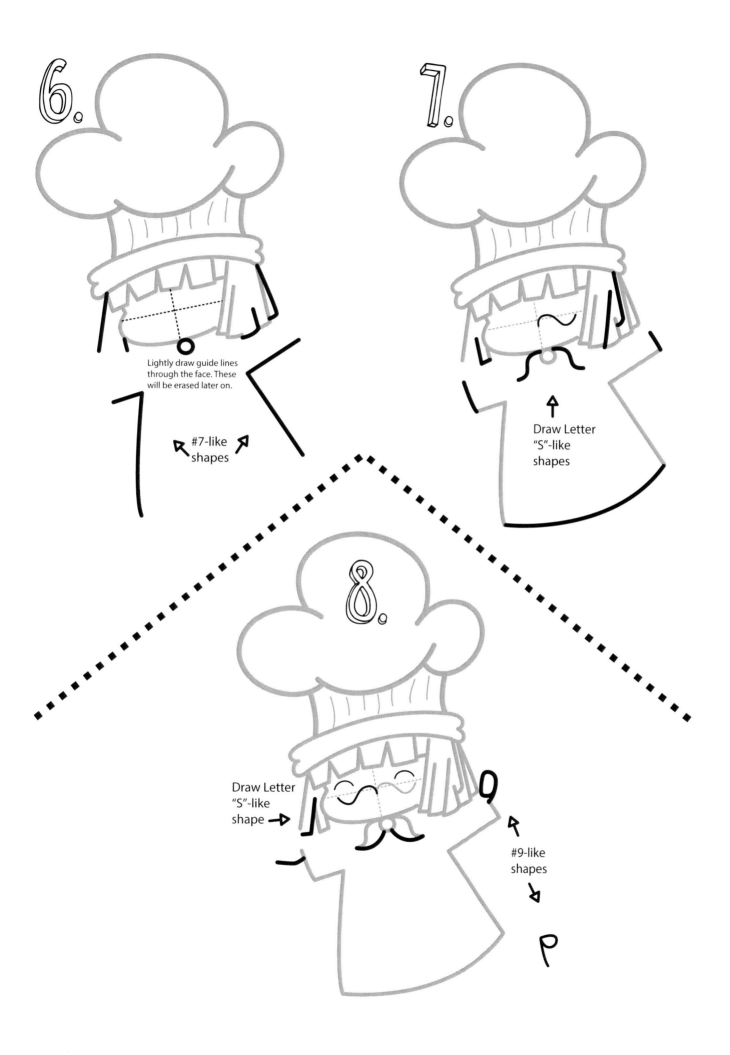

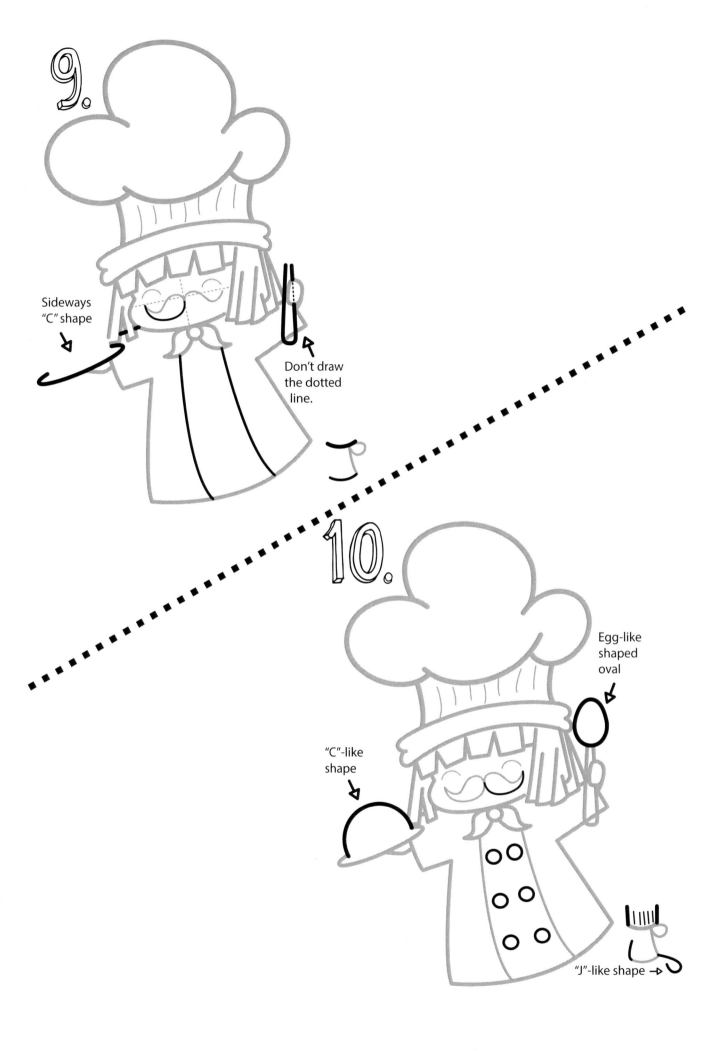

CUTE PIRATES

1.

2.

Lightly draw guide lines through the face. These will be erased later on.

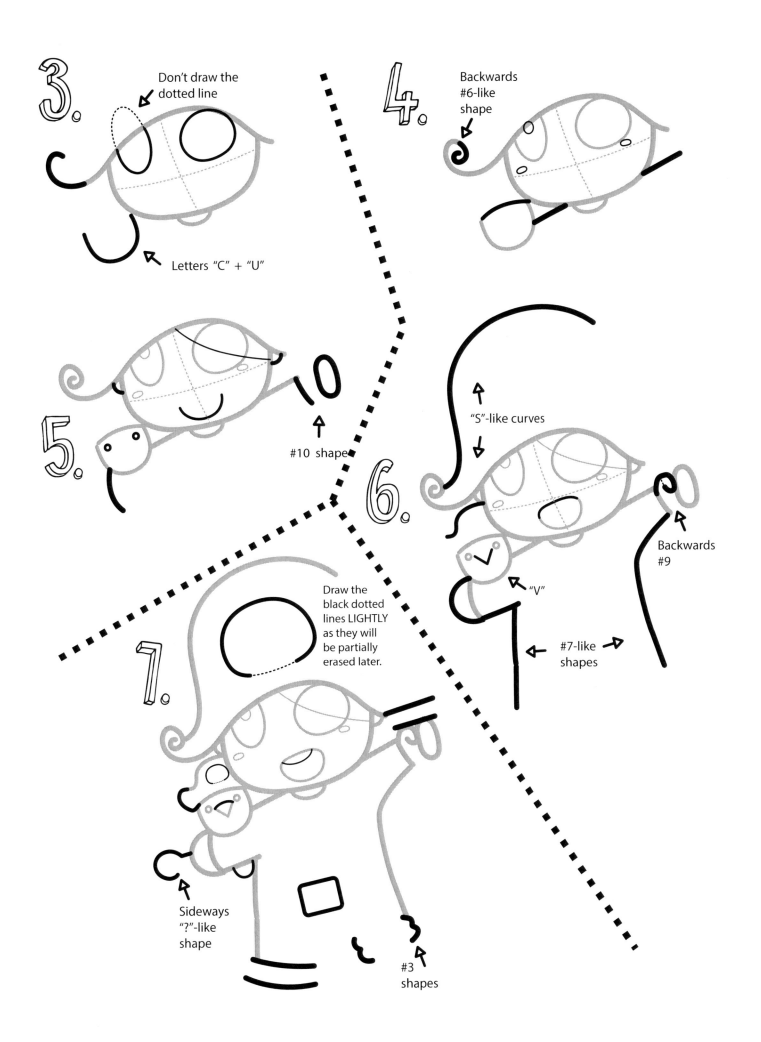

CUTE DRAGONS

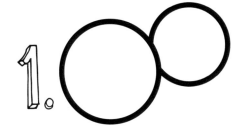

1. Draw a slanted #8 shape.

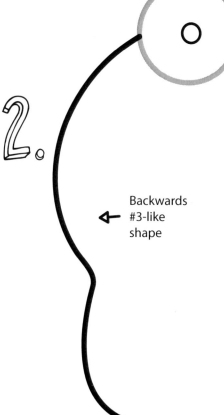

2. Backwards #3-like shape

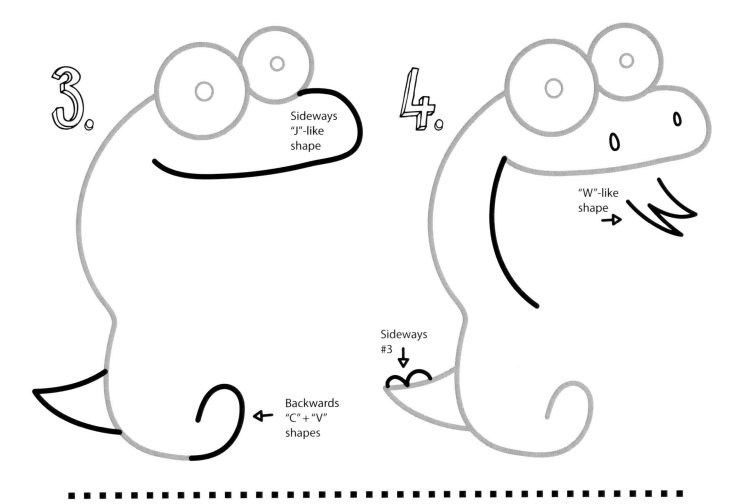
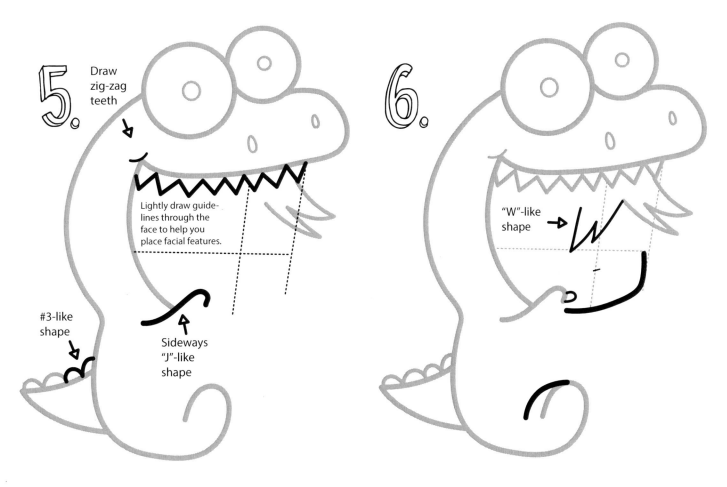

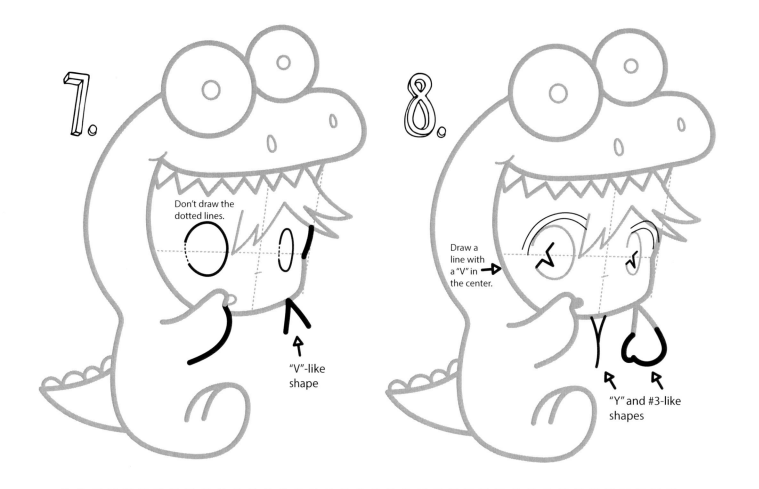
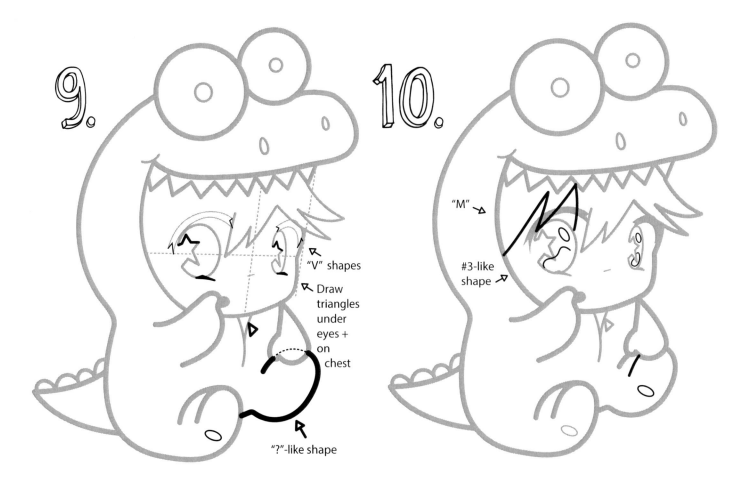

NOW FOR THE TINY DRAGON

A. Draw some #3-like shapes

B. #7-like shape

C. Draw some "U" and #3-Like shapes / Draw a sideways "S" curve

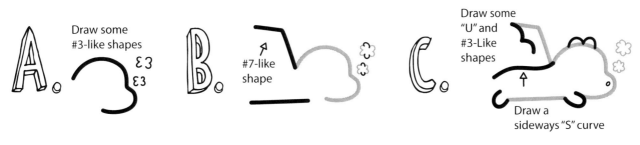

D. #3 / #7

E. Draw #3 shaped humps / "V"

F.

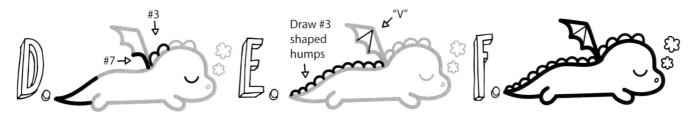

CUTE SUPER HEROES

1. Lightly draw a rectangle-like shape that is slightly wider at the top. These lines will be erased later.

2. Lightly draw lines through it, as I have done.

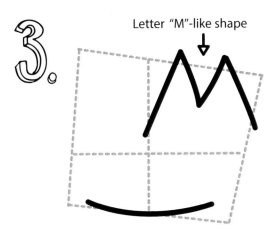
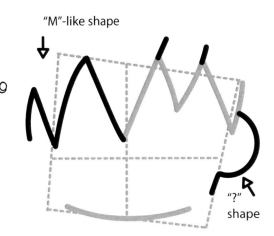
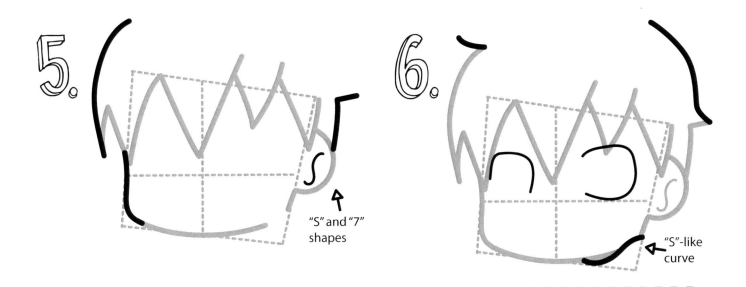
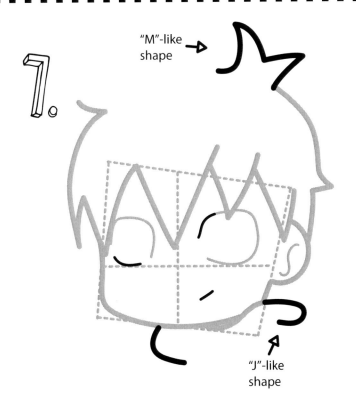

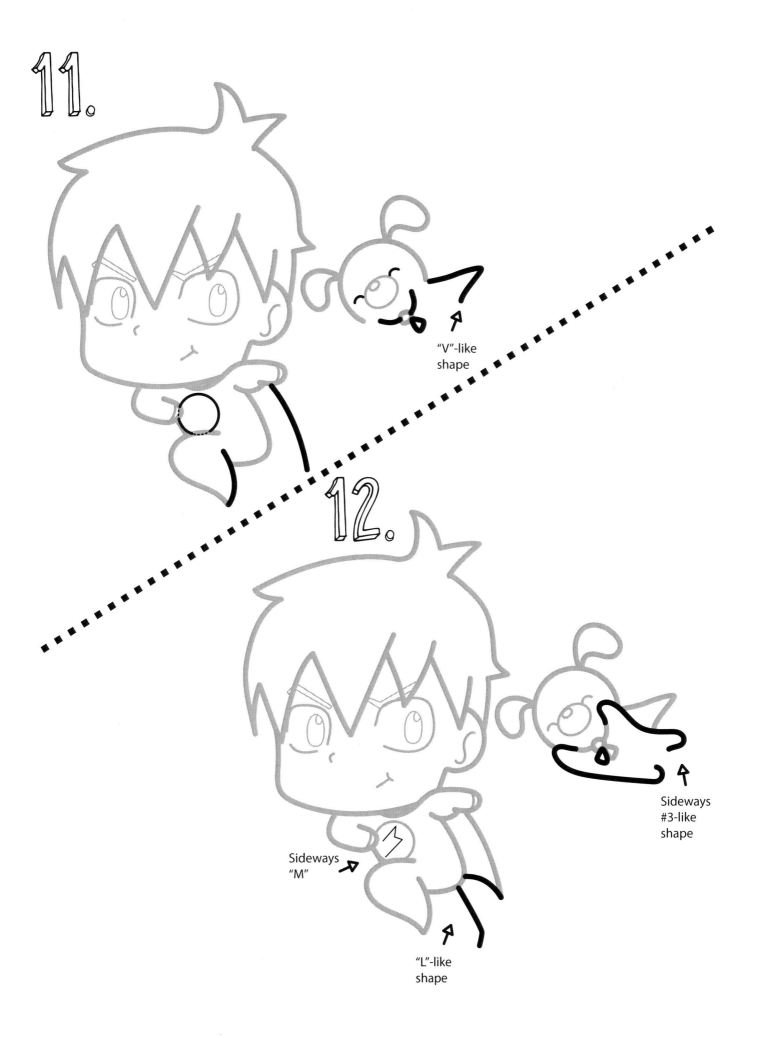

LITTLE HUNGRY MICE

1. Draw an odd-shaped oval.

2. Draw a triangle and a curved line.

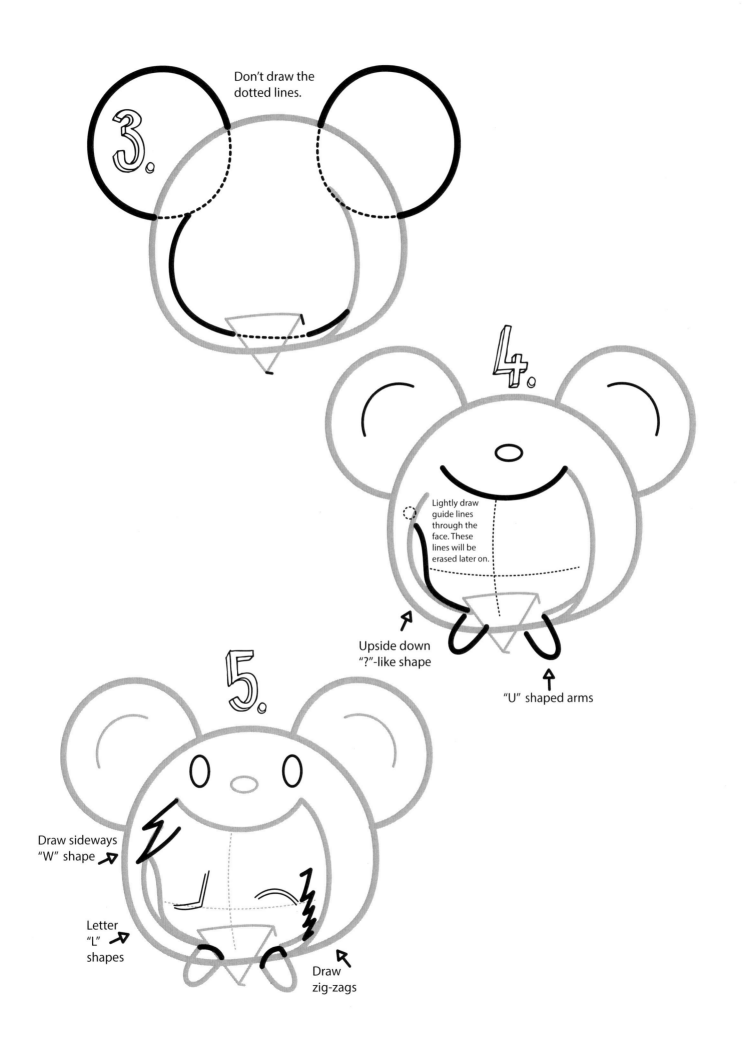

SLEEPY TIME

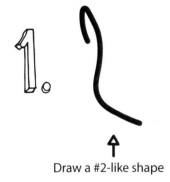

1.

↑
Draw a #2-like shape

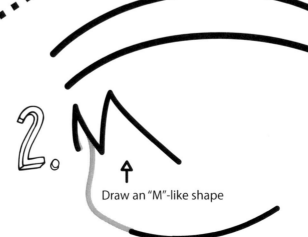

2.

↑
Draw an "M"-like shape

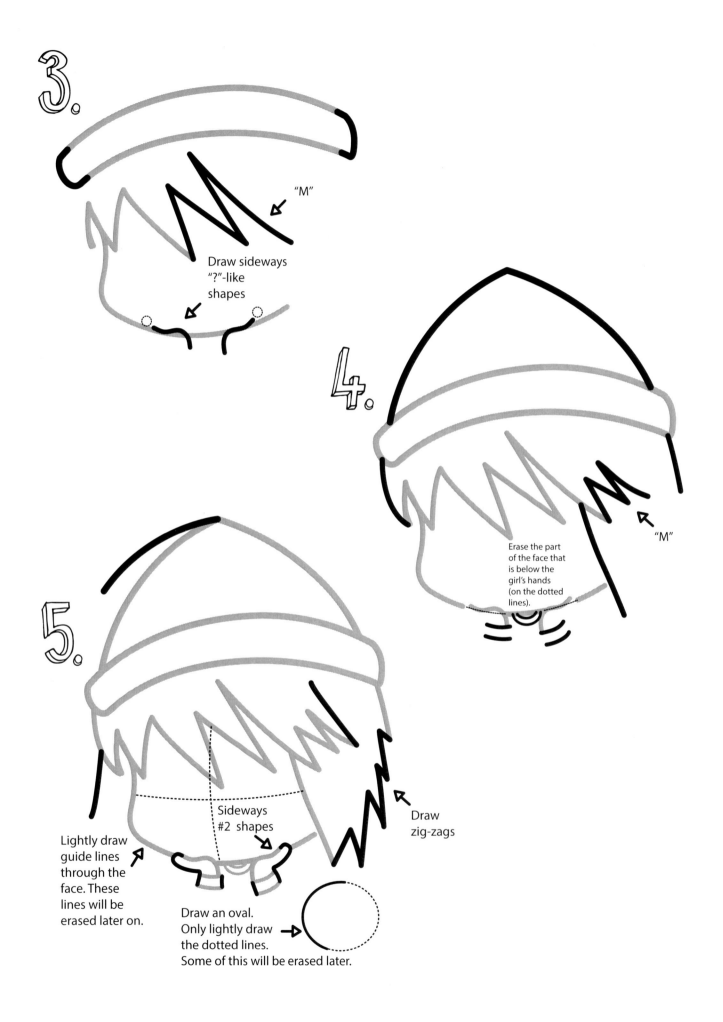

Draw cloud shapes at the end of their caps.

RIBBON DANCERS

1.

2. "V" and "N"-like shapes

Lightly draw guide lines through the face. These lines will be erased later on.

Draw a backwards "?"-like shape →

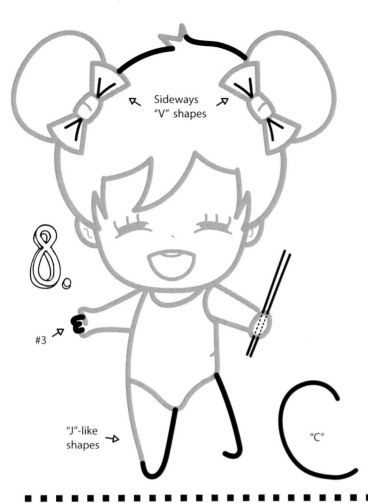

10.

"U" shapes

11.

Follow the curve of previous line

"?"-like shapes

HUNGRY SHARK

1. Start off with a slanted letter "C" shape. This will be the shark's mouth.

2. Draw letter "V" shapes all along the shark's mouth. These will be the shark's teeth.

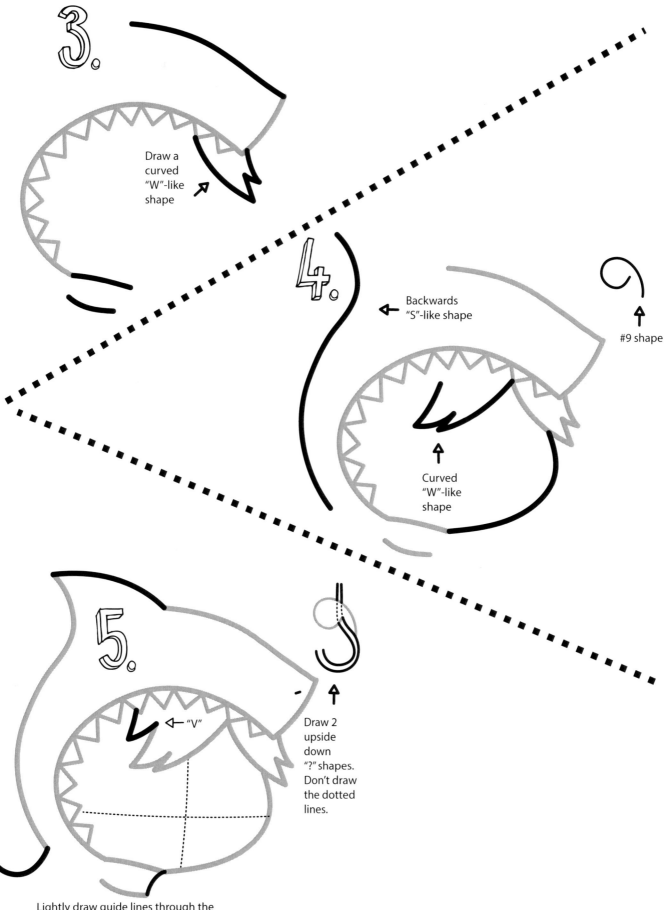

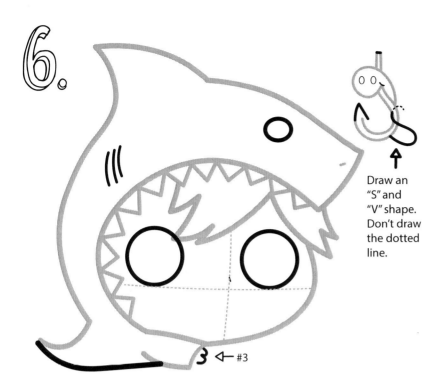

Draw an "S" and "V" shape. Don't draw the dotted line.

← #3

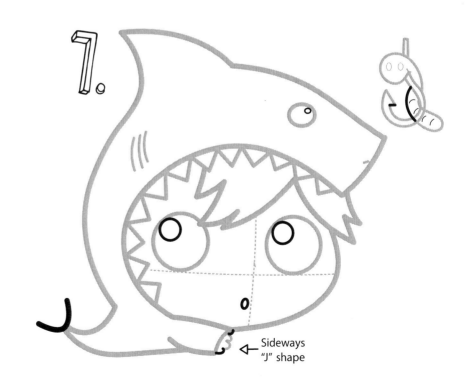

← Sideways "J" shape

8.

Erase on the dotted lines

9.

CUTESY MERMAID

1. Lightly draw an oval shaped guide line. Most of this will be erased later on.

2. Use the guide line to help guide you in drawing this curved line.

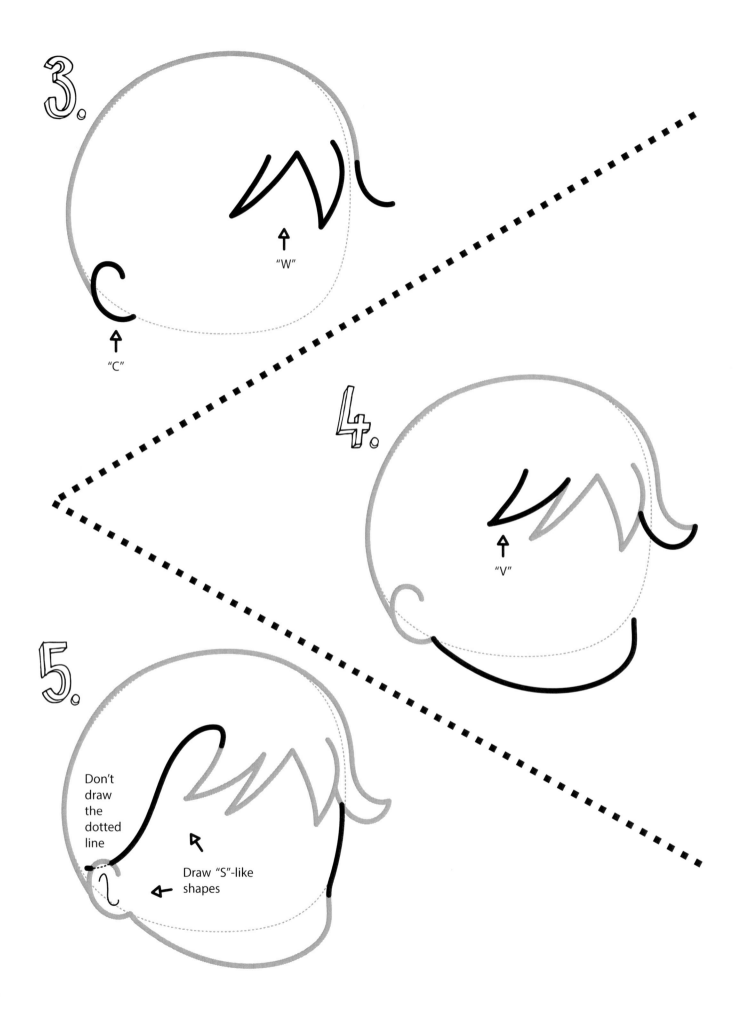

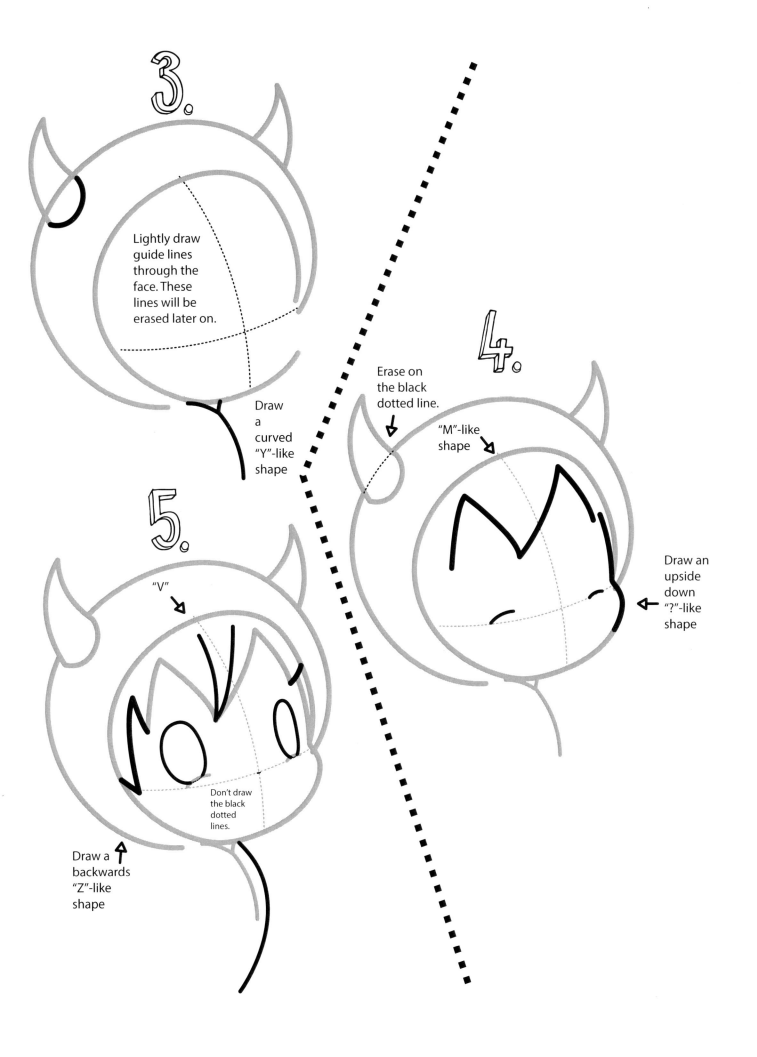

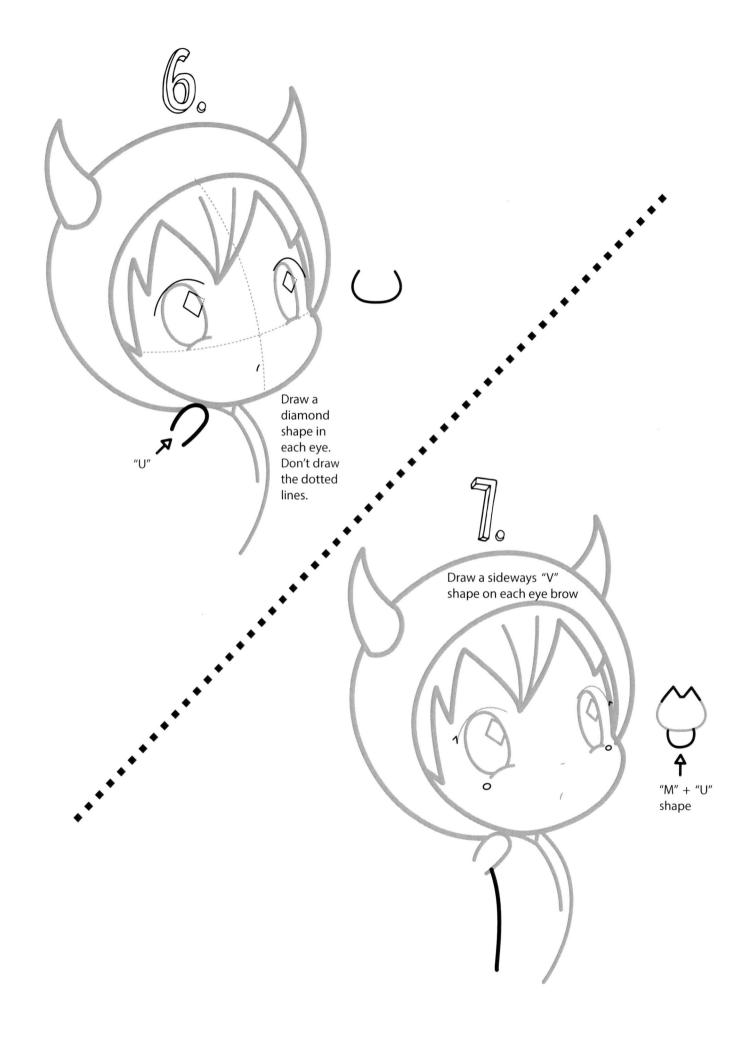

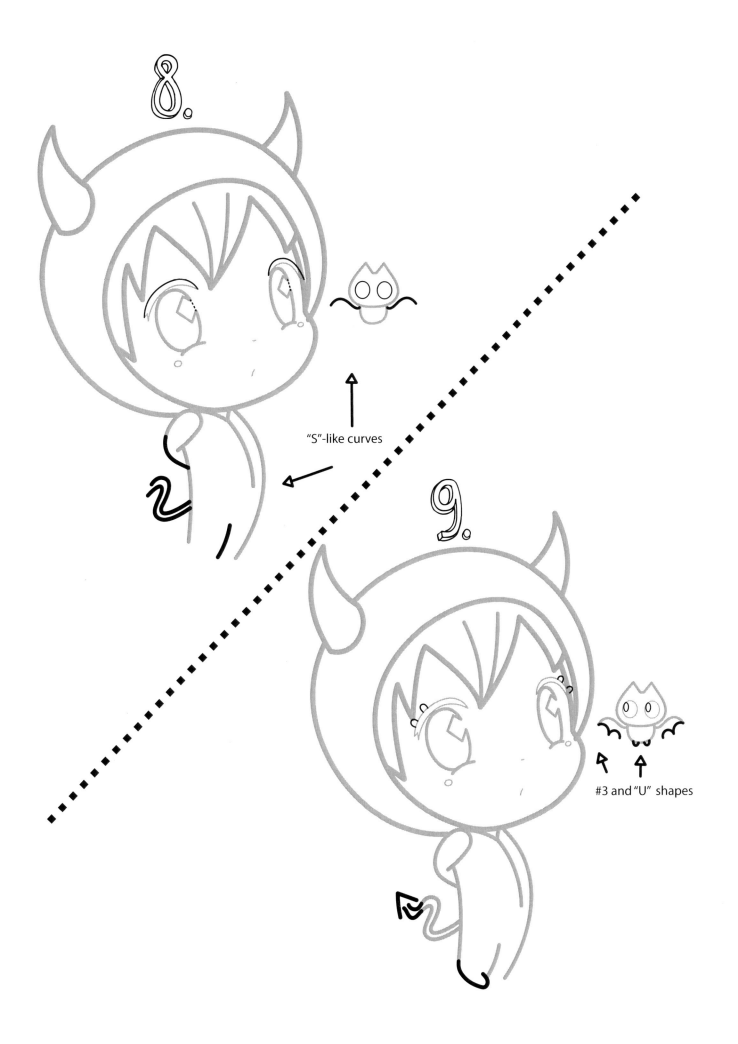

MAIL TIME!!

1.

2. "W" →

"C" ↑

Lightly draw guide lines through the face. These lines will be erased later on.

Erase on the dotted line.

SPACE FRIENDS

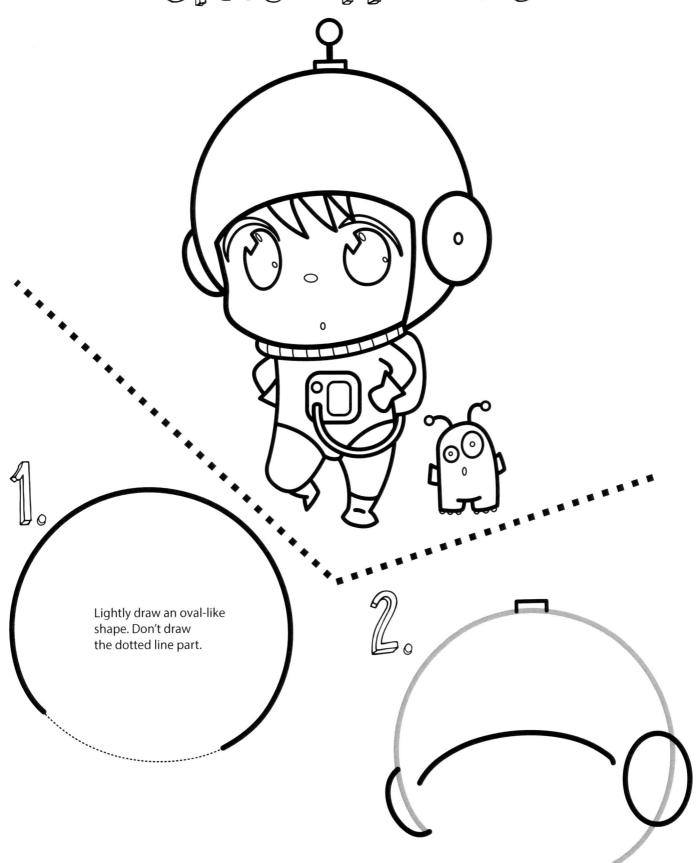

1. Lightly draw an oval-like shape. Don't draw the dotted line part.

2.

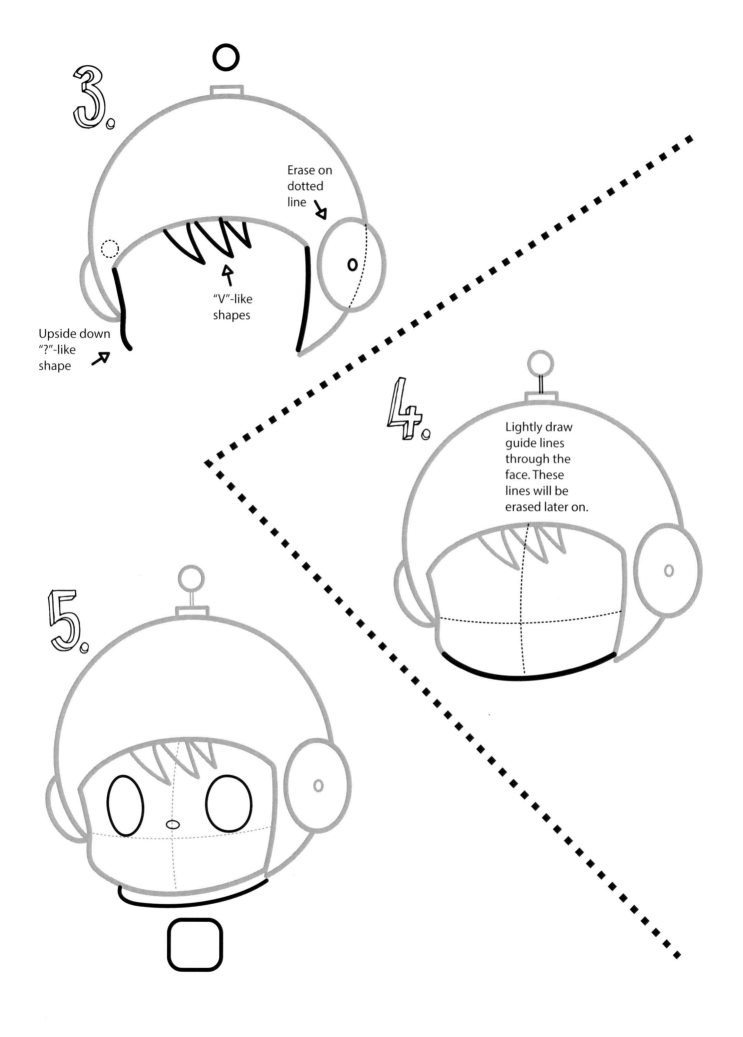

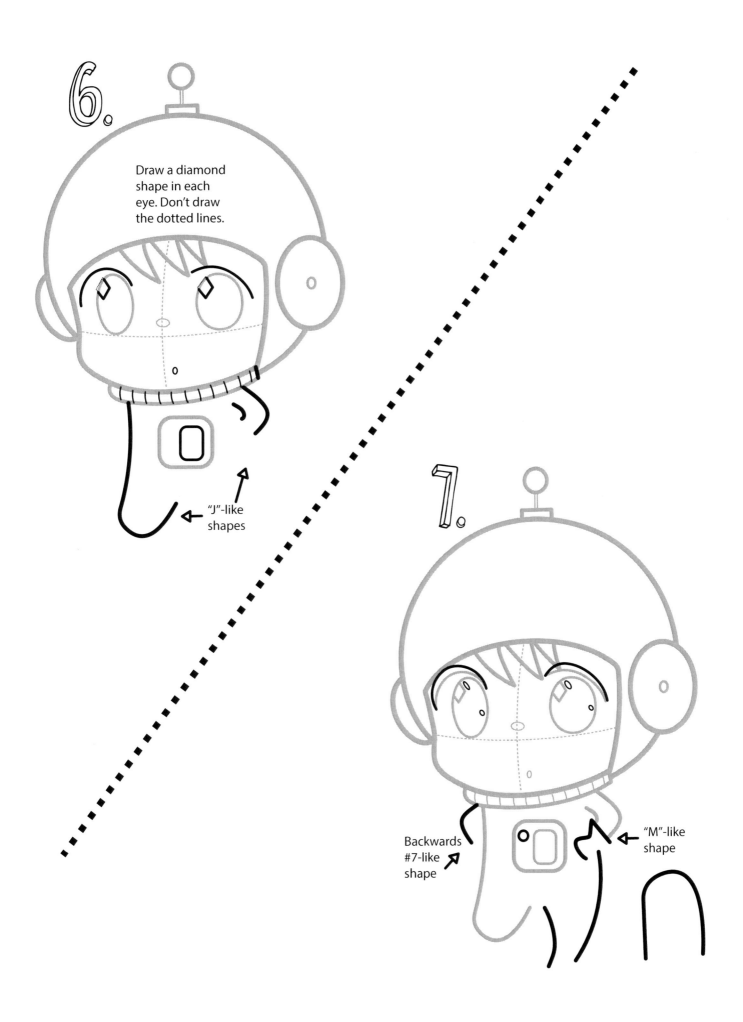

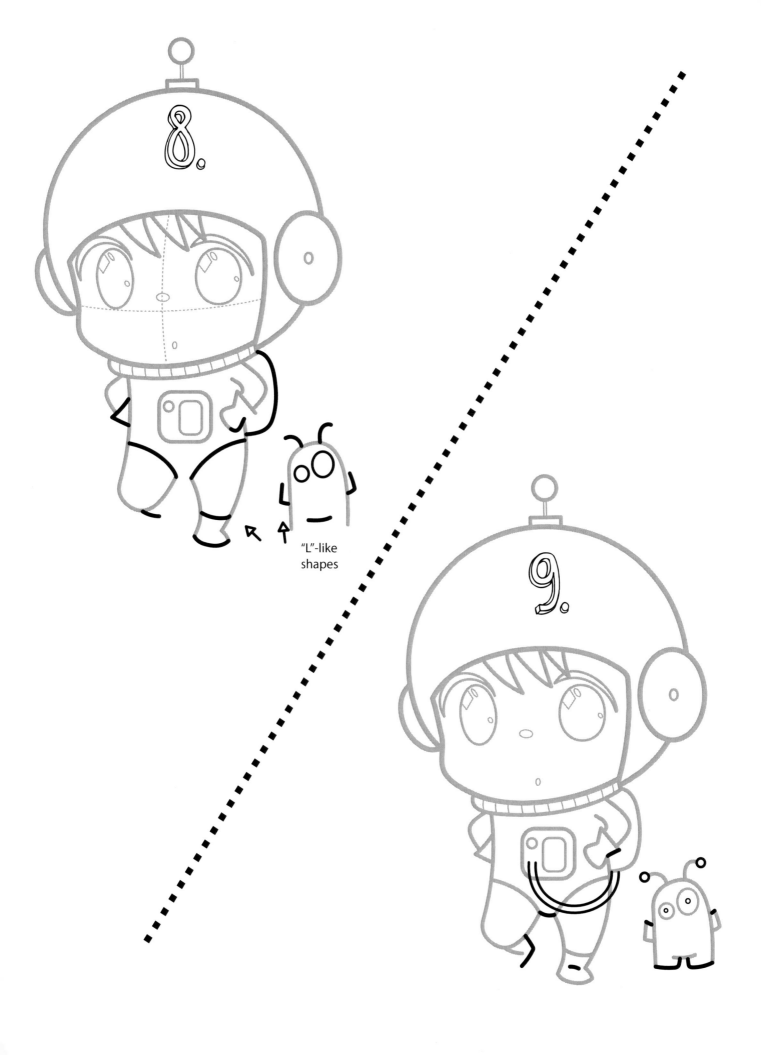

Erase on dotted lines

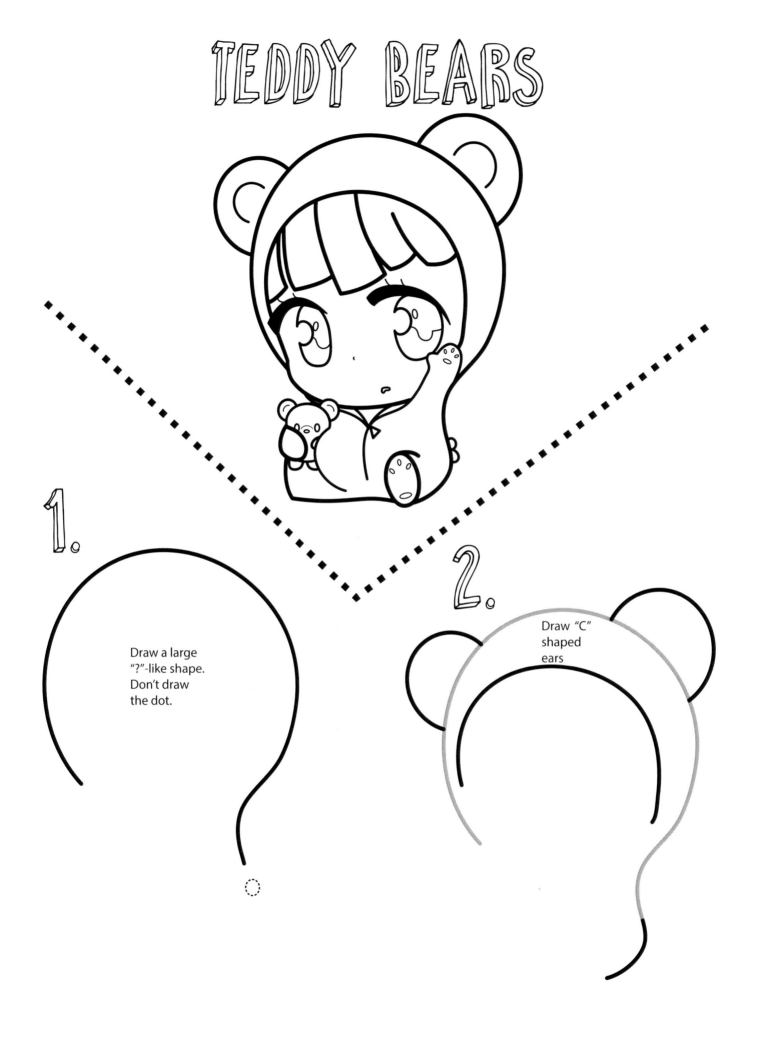

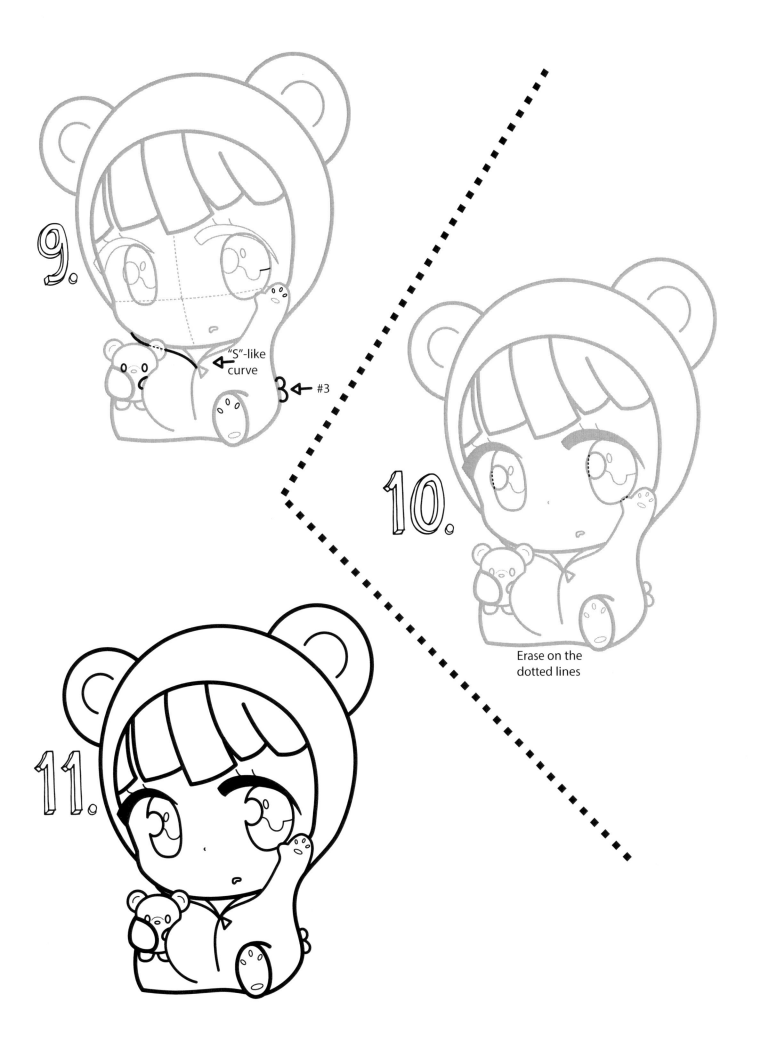

ADORABLE BUNNIES

■ ■

1. ○

2.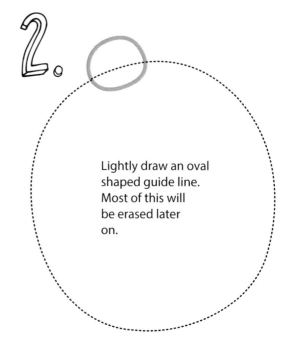

Lightly draw an oval shaped guide line. Most of this will be erased later on.

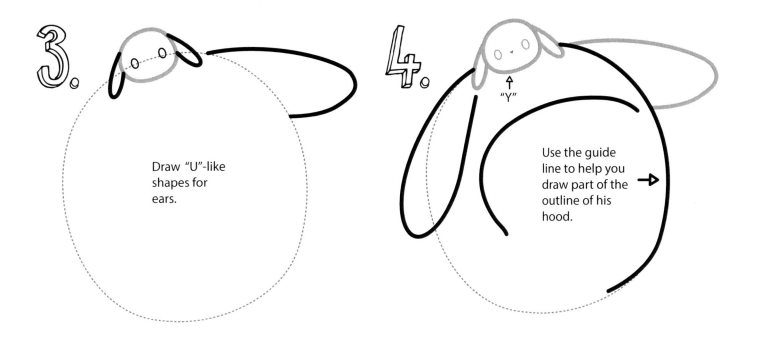

BUSY DOCTOR

....

1. Lightly draw an oval and a curved line for the face's guide lines.

2. Outline the right side of these guide lines. Erase the guide lines.

3. Lightly draw guide lines through the face. These lines will be erased later on.

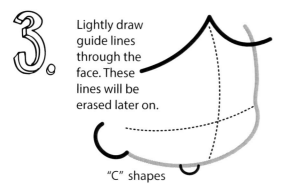

"C" shapes

4.

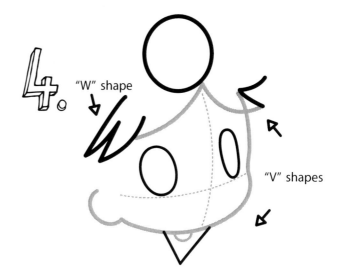

"W" shape

"V" shapes

5. Draw a diamond in each eye

Letter "V" + "L" shapes

6. Draw the curved lines, but don't draw the dotted lines.

Erase parts of the eyes that are dotted lines.

LITTLE ANGEL

1.

Draw a shape that sort of looks like a sideways "?" shape. Don't draw the dot.

2. Draw a curvy "V"-like shape

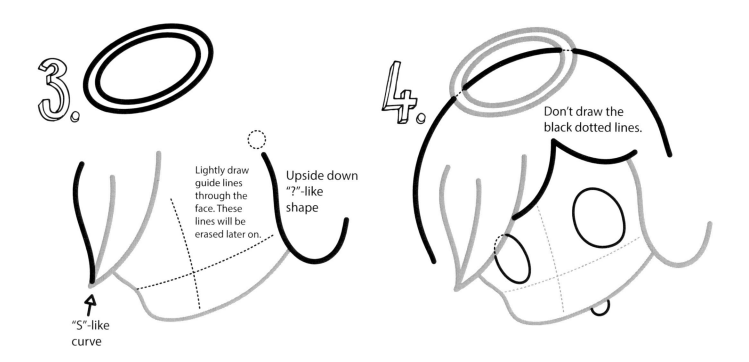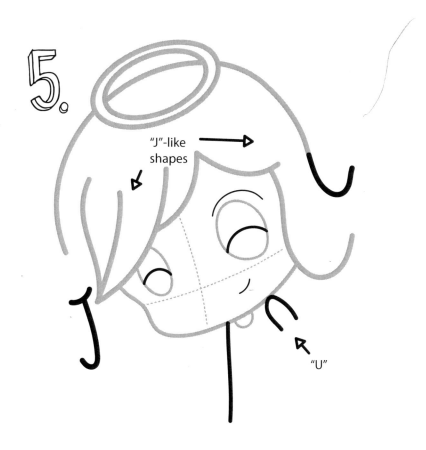

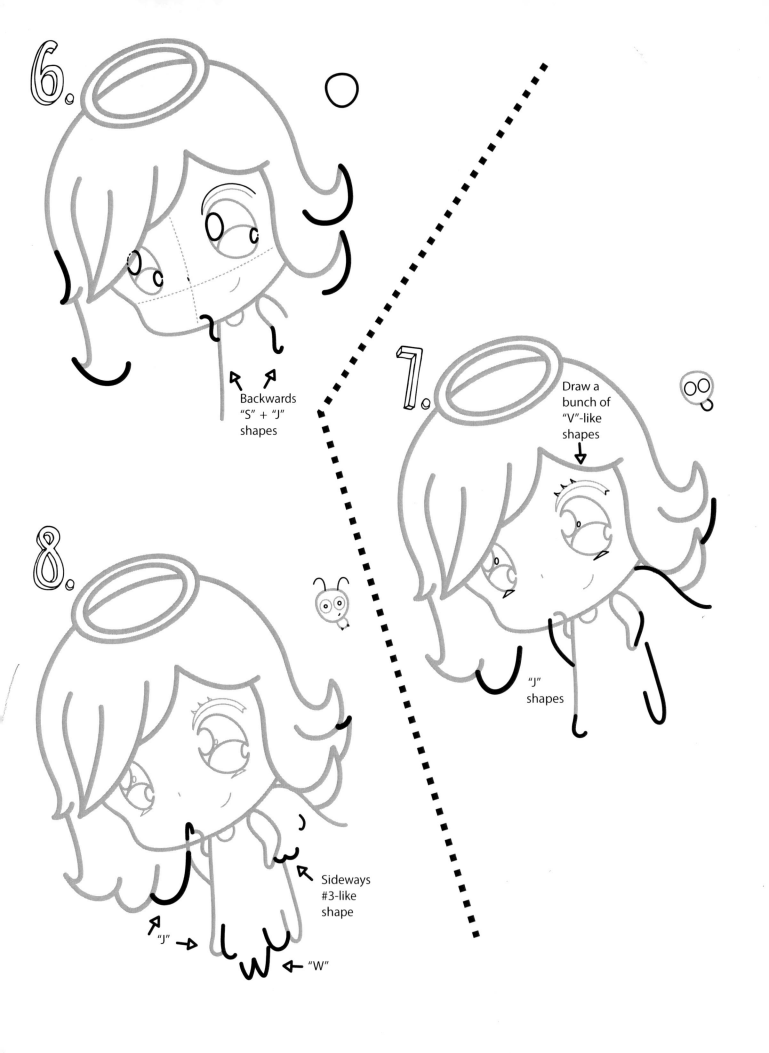

CUTE FOOTBALLER

1. Draw an oval. Don't draw the dotted line.

2. Draw an "S"-like shape

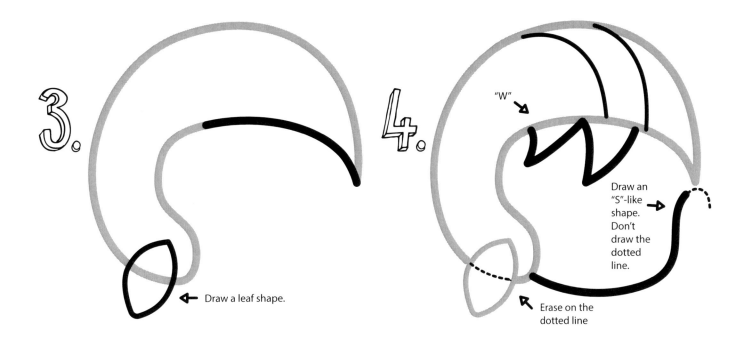
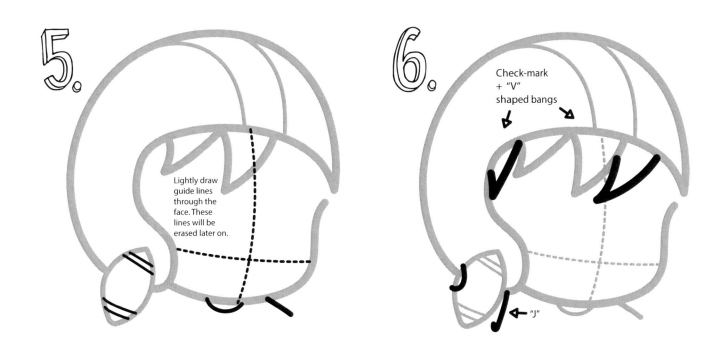

CUTE RACCOONS

1. Lightly draw a rectangle with lines through it. These will guide you through drawing the face and will be erased later on.

2. Draw an upside down "?"-like shape. Don't draw the dot.

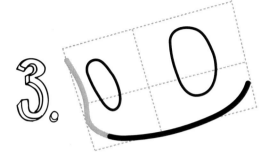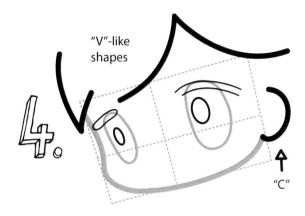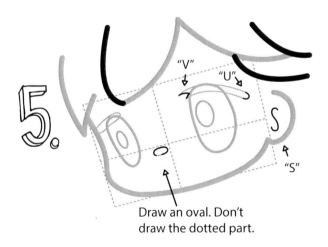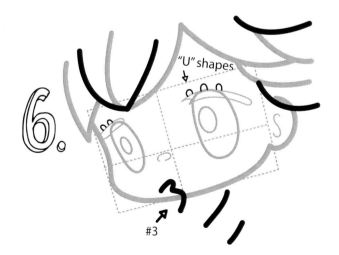

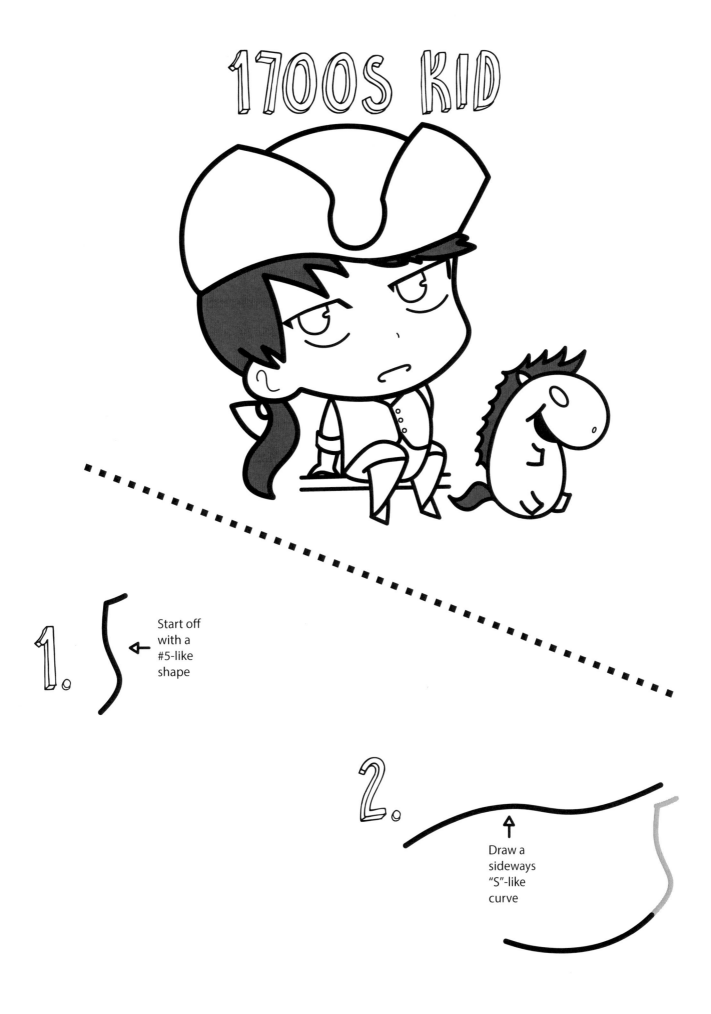

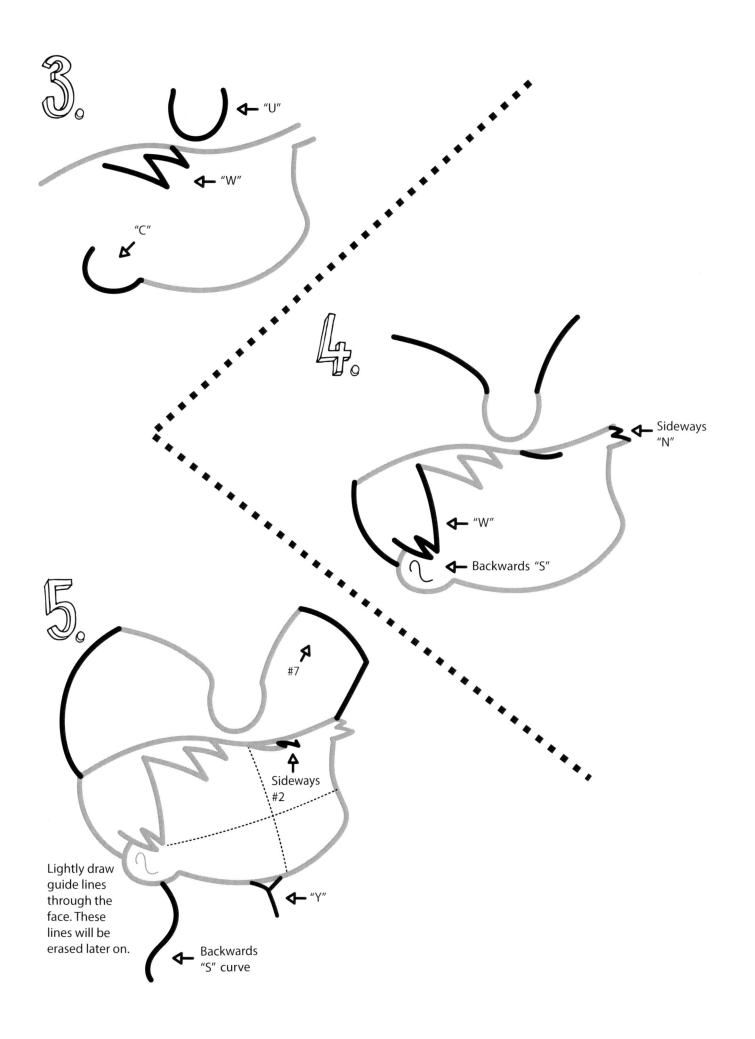

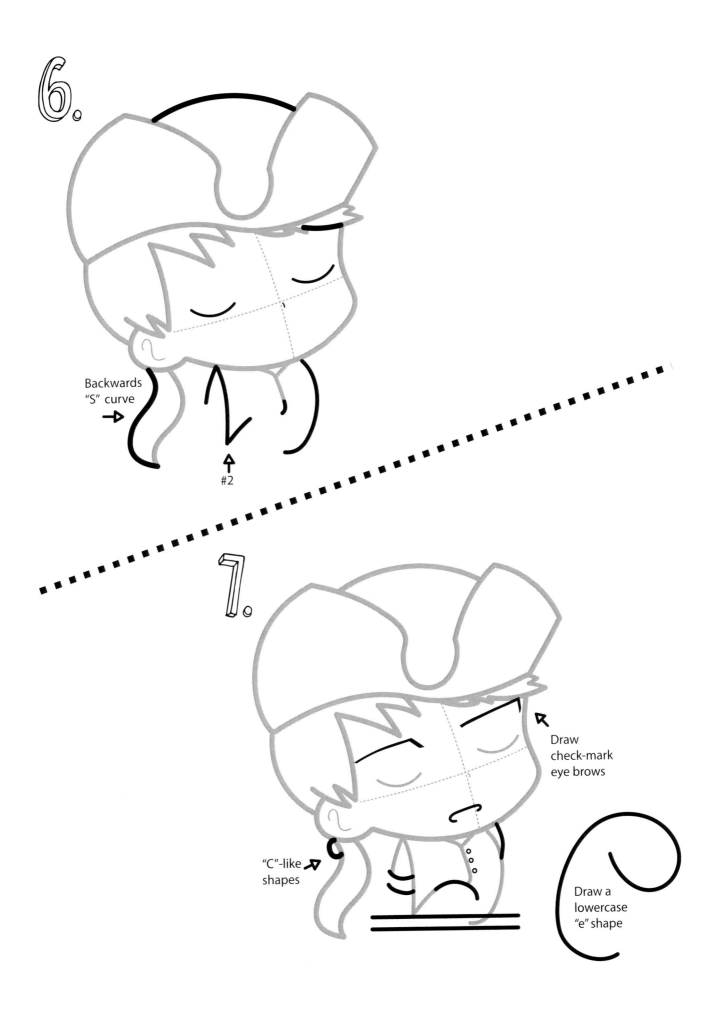

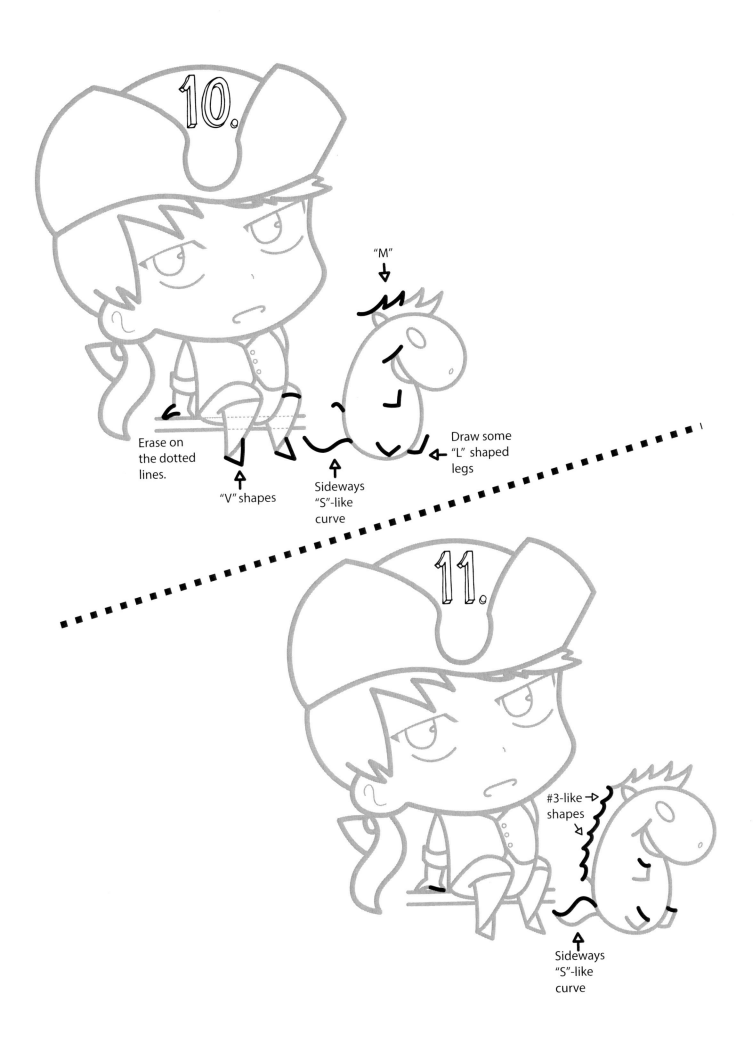

BABY UNICORNS

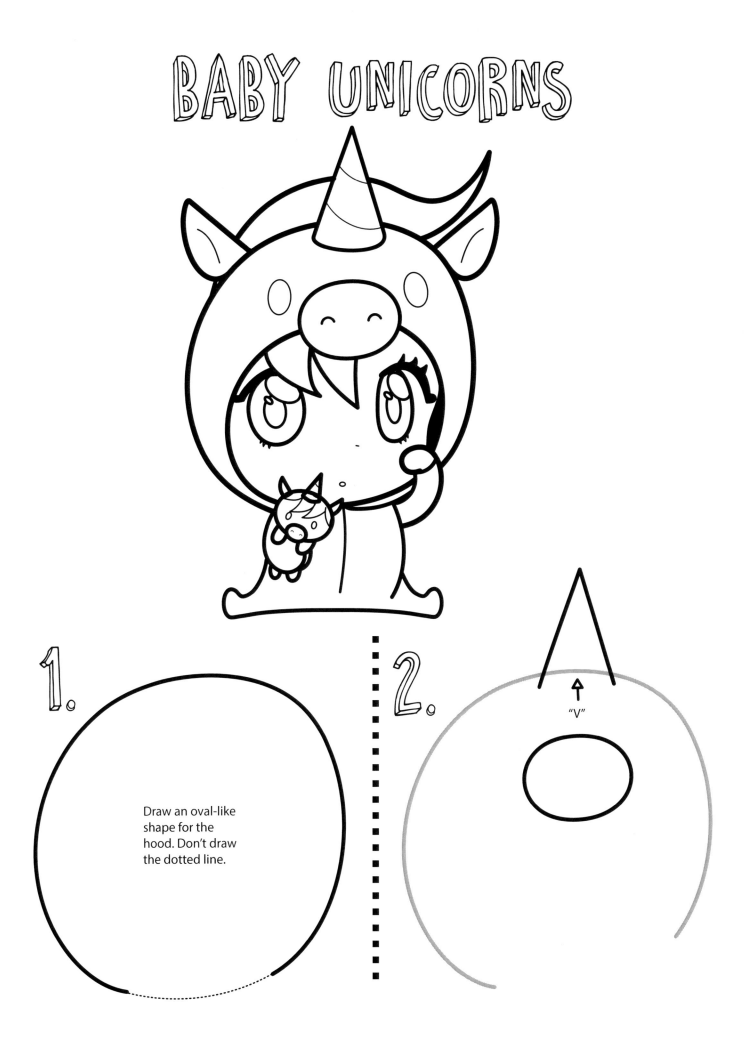

1. Draw an oval-like shape for the hood. Don't draw the dotted line.

2. "V"

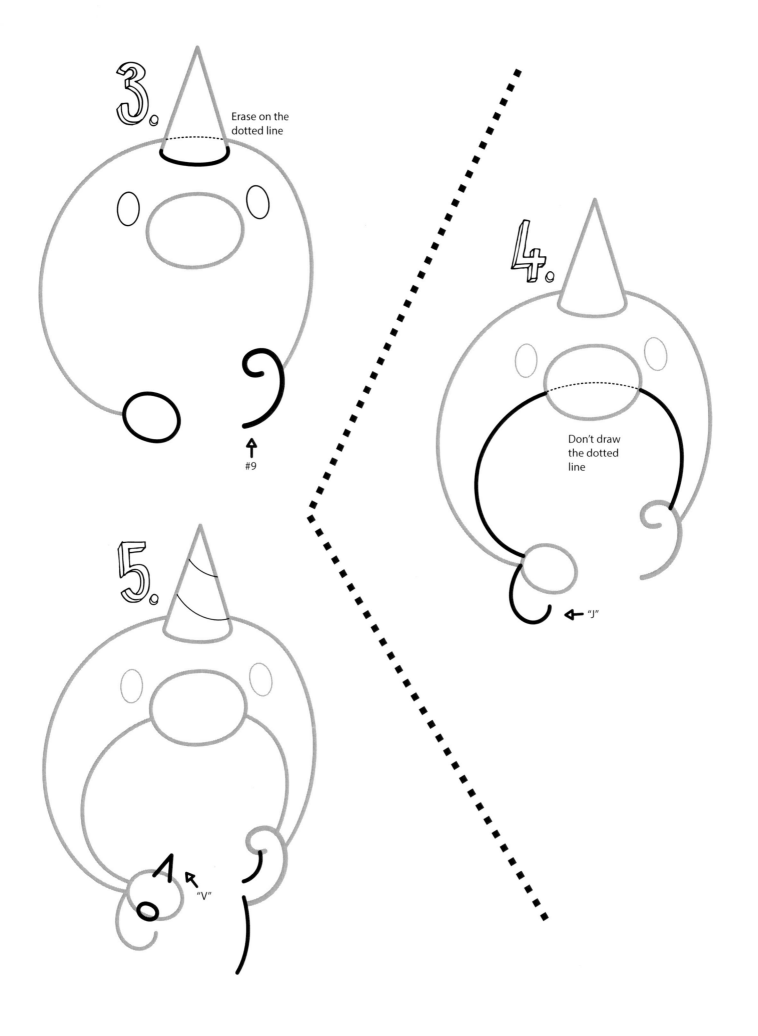

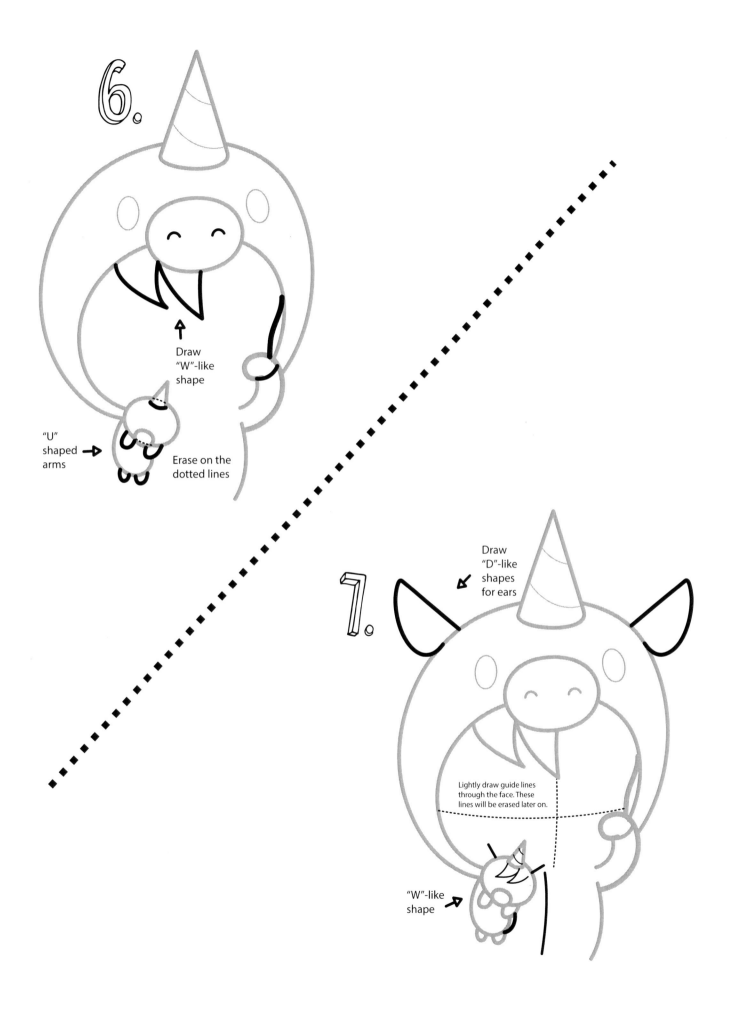

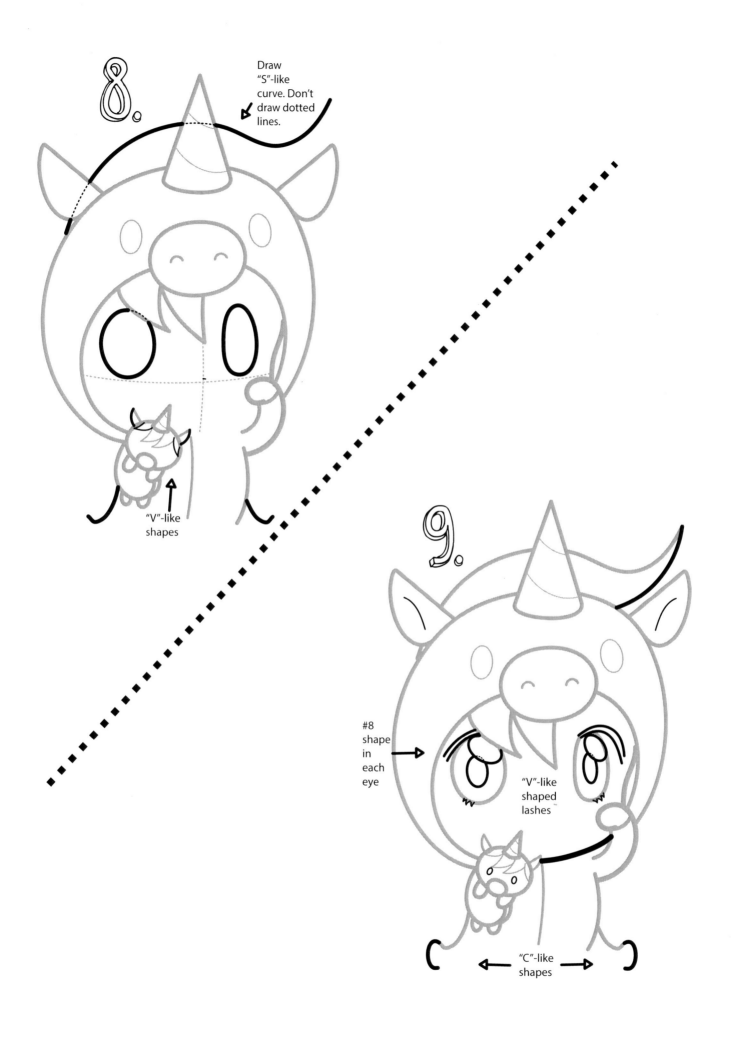

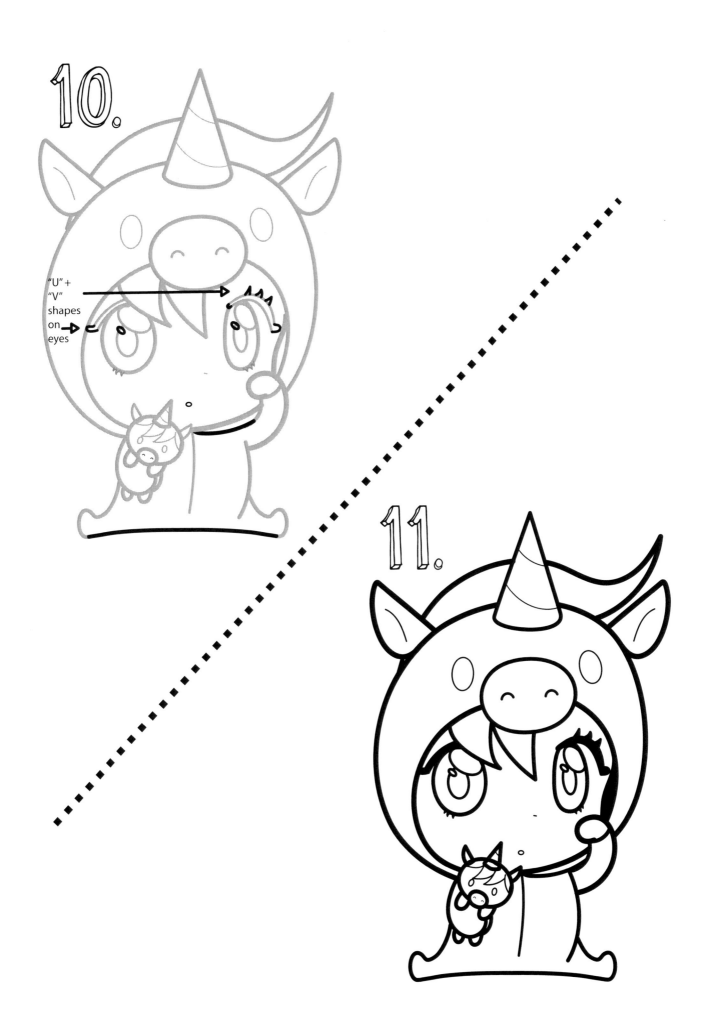

LITTLE COWGIRL

1. Lightly draw an oval shaped guide line. Most of this will be erased later on.

2. Draw a sideways "S"-like curve

Lightly draw guide lines through the oval. These lines will be erased later on.

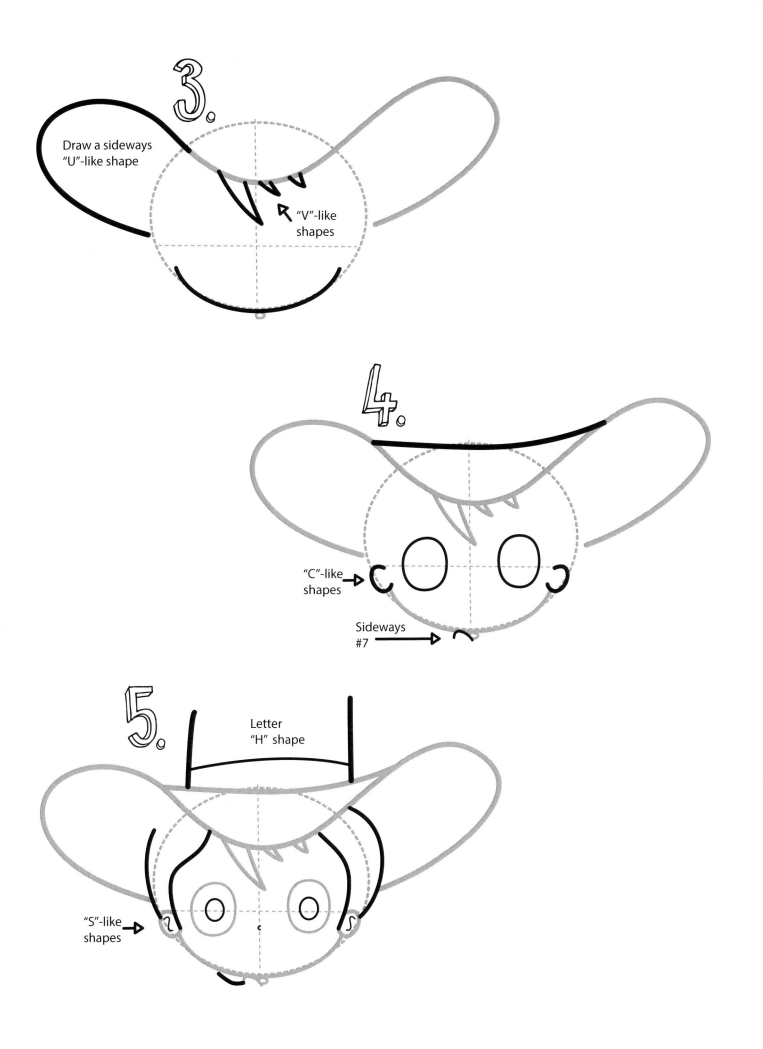

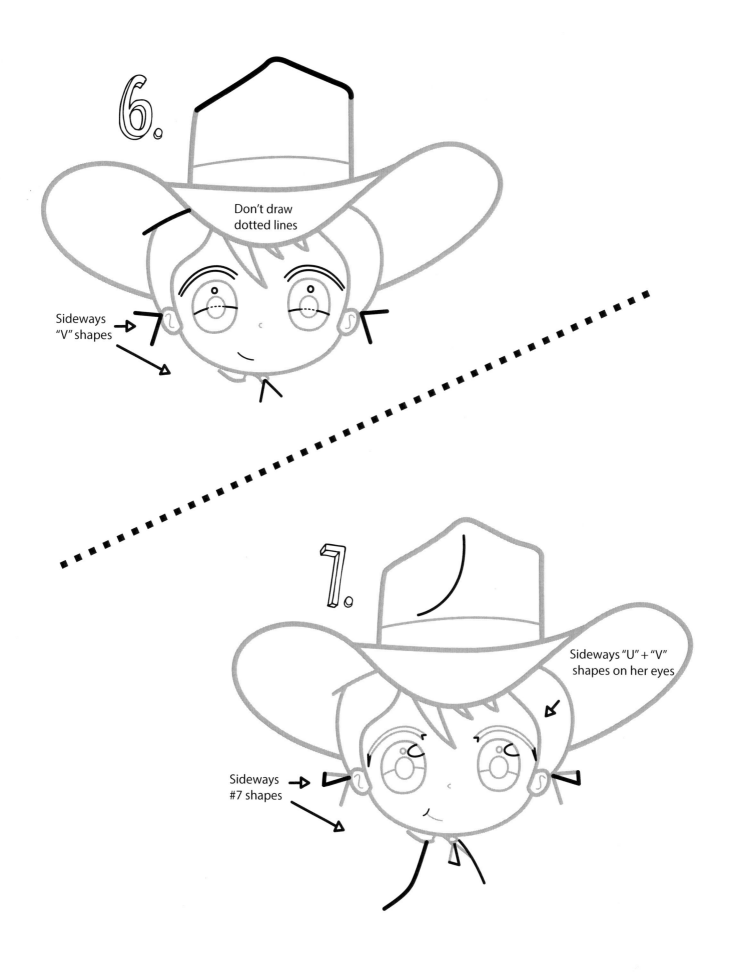

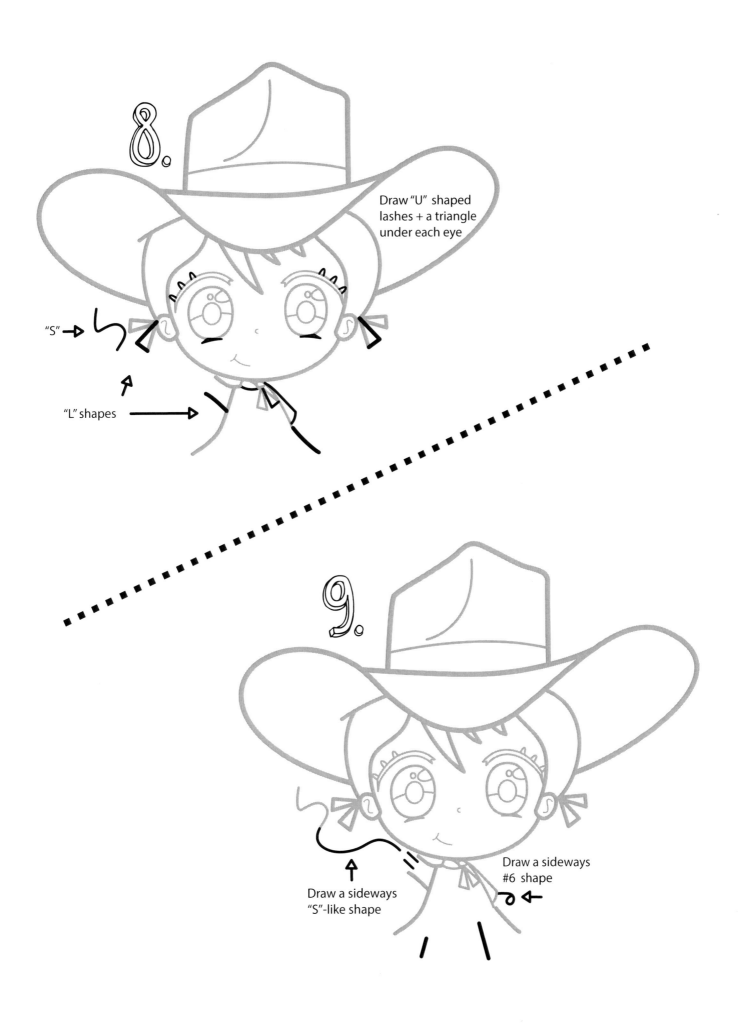

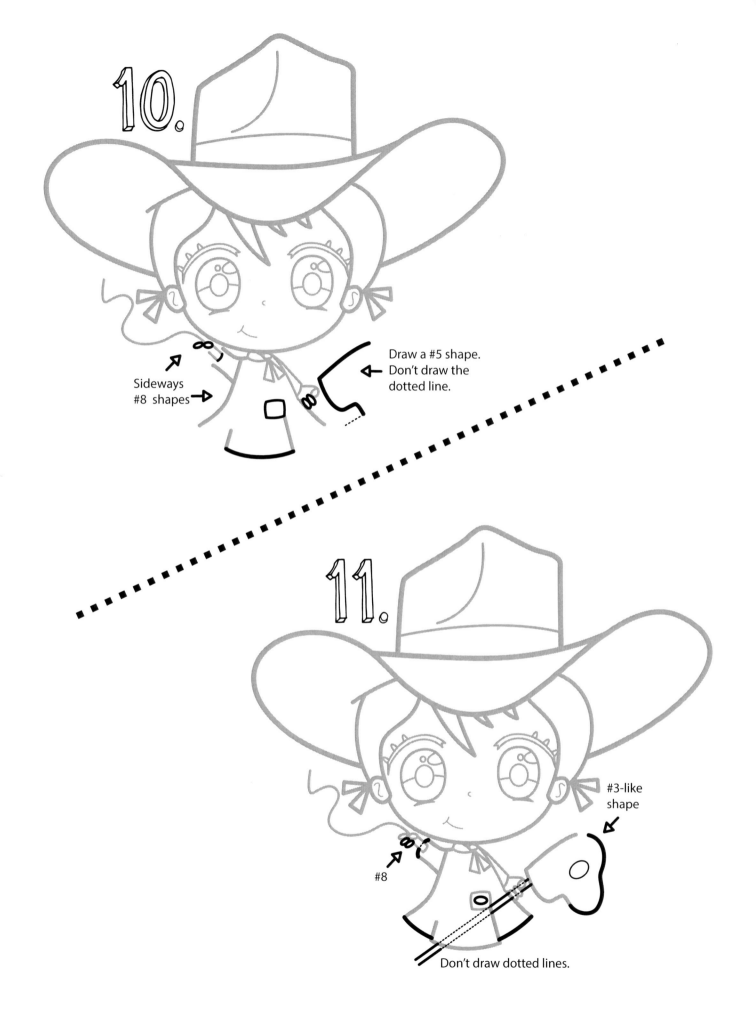

SCARY SKELETONS

1. Lightly draw an oval and a rectangle for the face's guide lines. These lines will be erased later on.

2. Lightly draw a line through it. This line will be erased later on.

Use the guide lines to help you place the facial features.

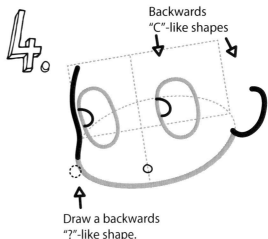

Backwards "C"-like shapes

Draw a backwards "?"-like shape. (Don't draw the dot)

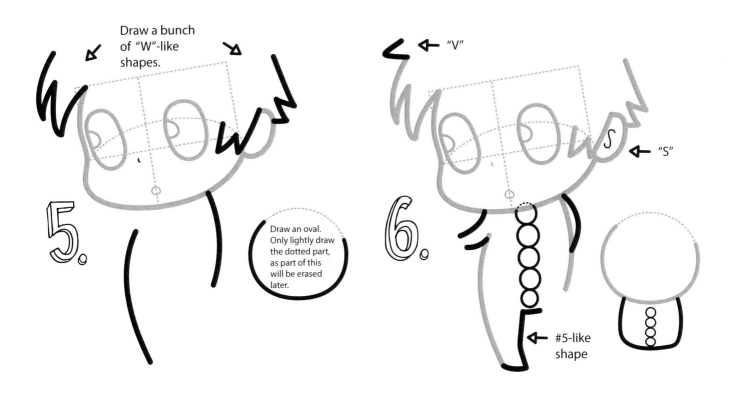

Draw a bunch of "W"-like shapes.

Draw an oval. Only lightly draw the dotted part, as part of this will be erased later.

"V"

"S"

#5-like shape

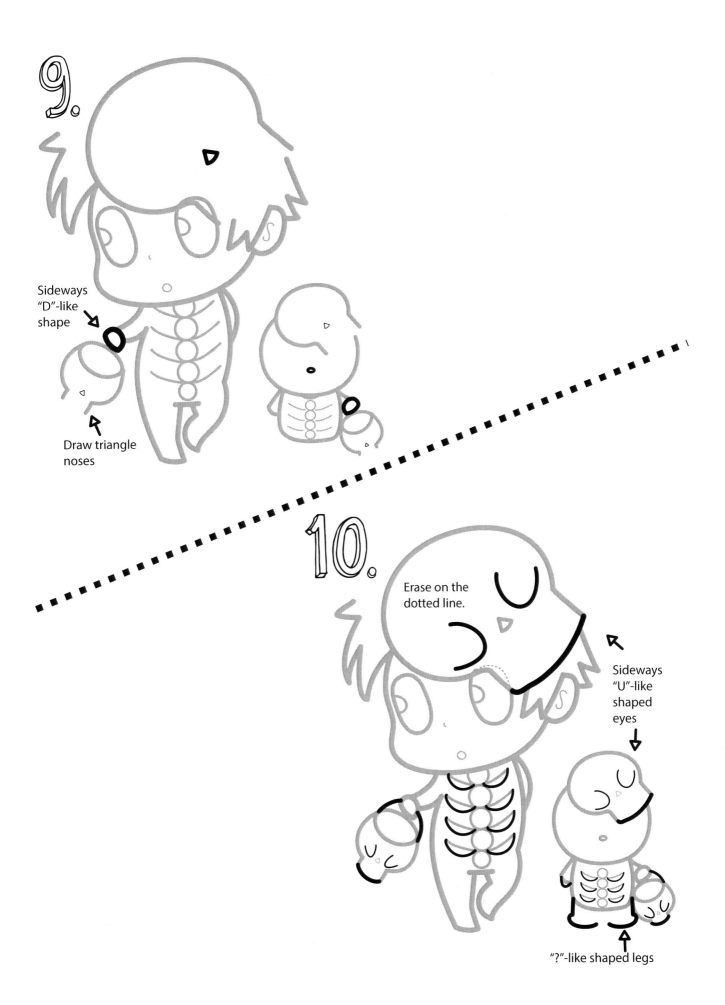

13.

CUTE DETECTIVES

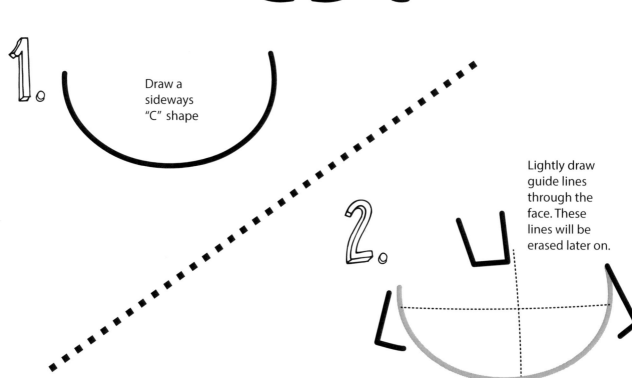

1. Draw a sideways "C" shape

2. Lightly draw guide lines through the face. These lines will be erased later on.

"L" shapes

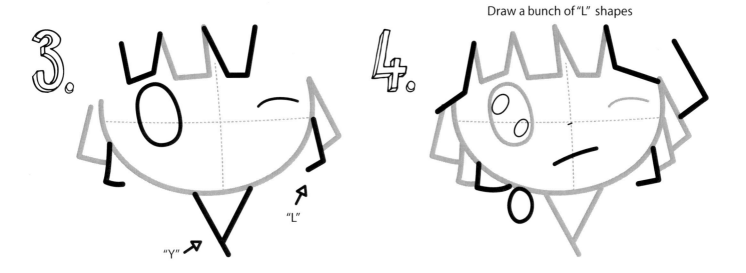
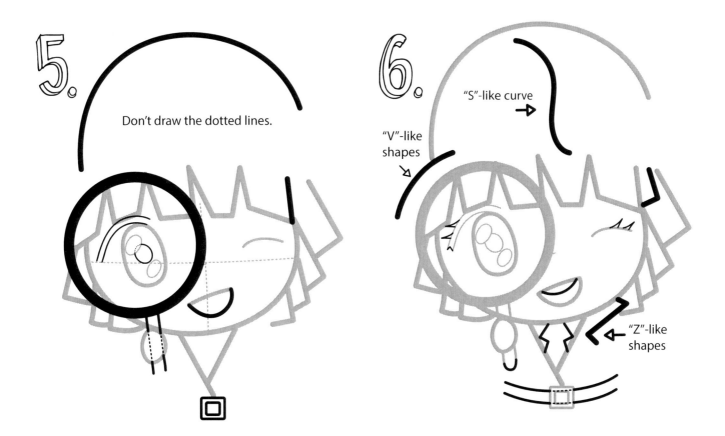

MARATHON RUNNERS

1. Draw a tiny "J" shape

2.

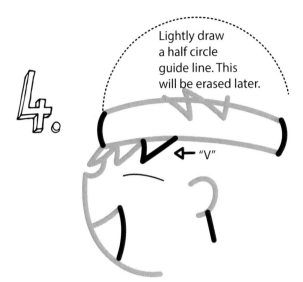

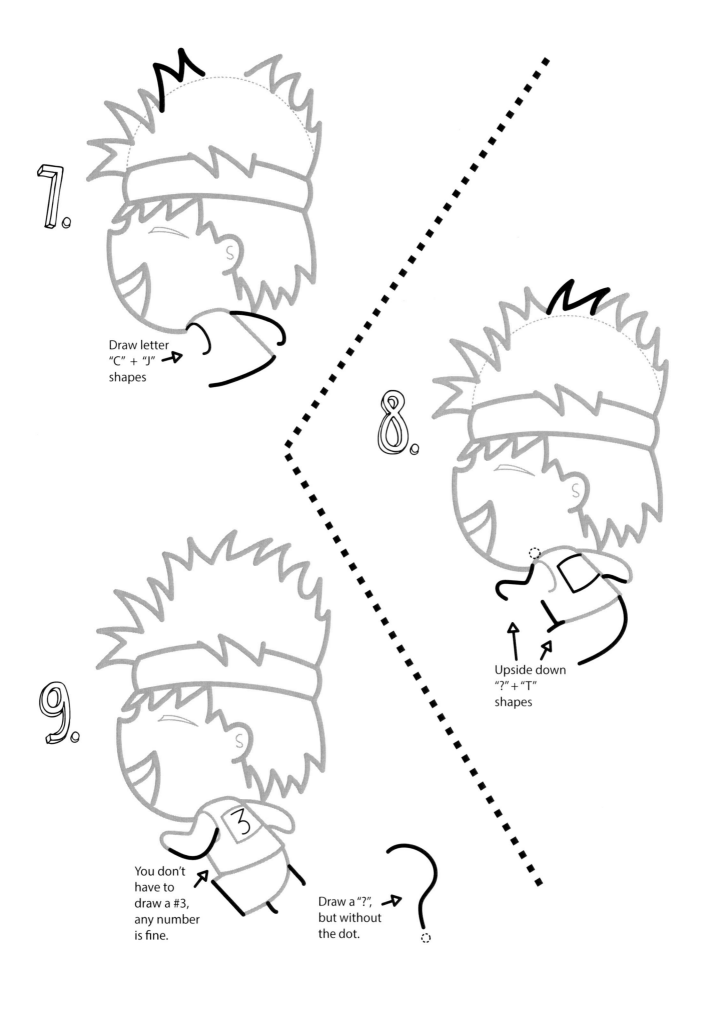

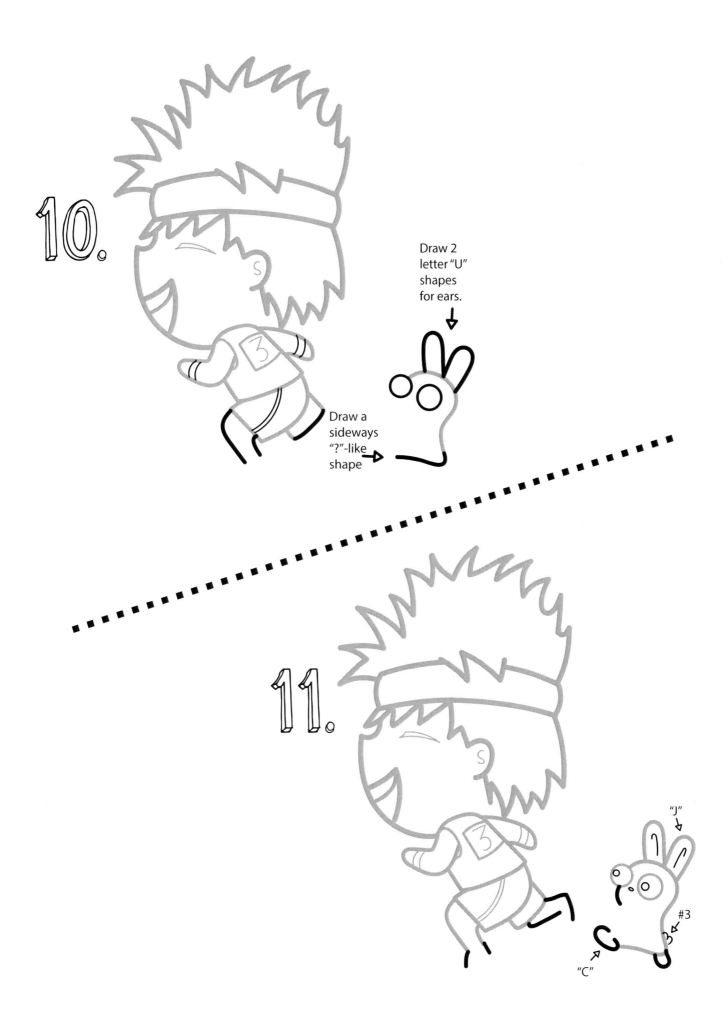

PEACEFUL MEDITATORS

1. Draw an upside down "?"-like shape. Don't draw the dotted circle.

2. "W"-like shape + a check-mark shape

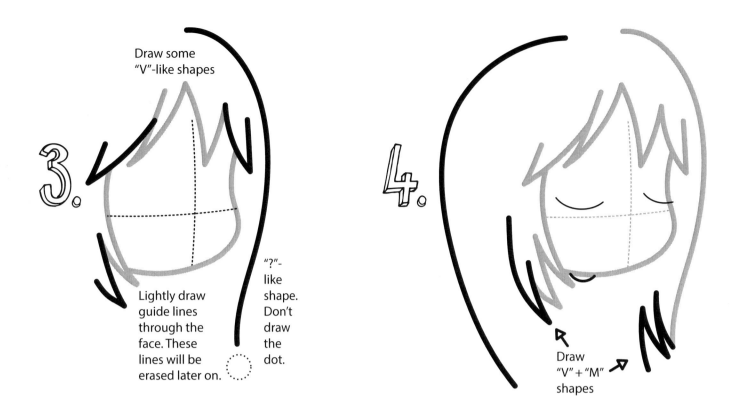

FISHING TIME

1.
Draw 2 curved lines that get closer together at the top.

2.
Draw an "S" curve. Lightly draw the dotted line.

"C" shape

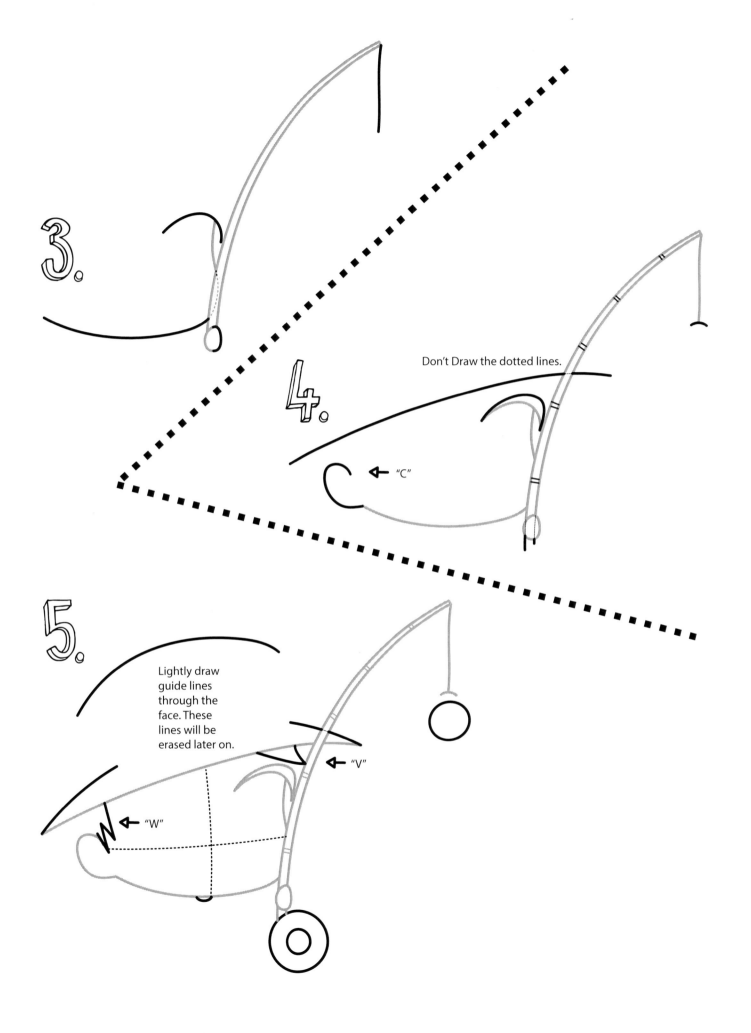

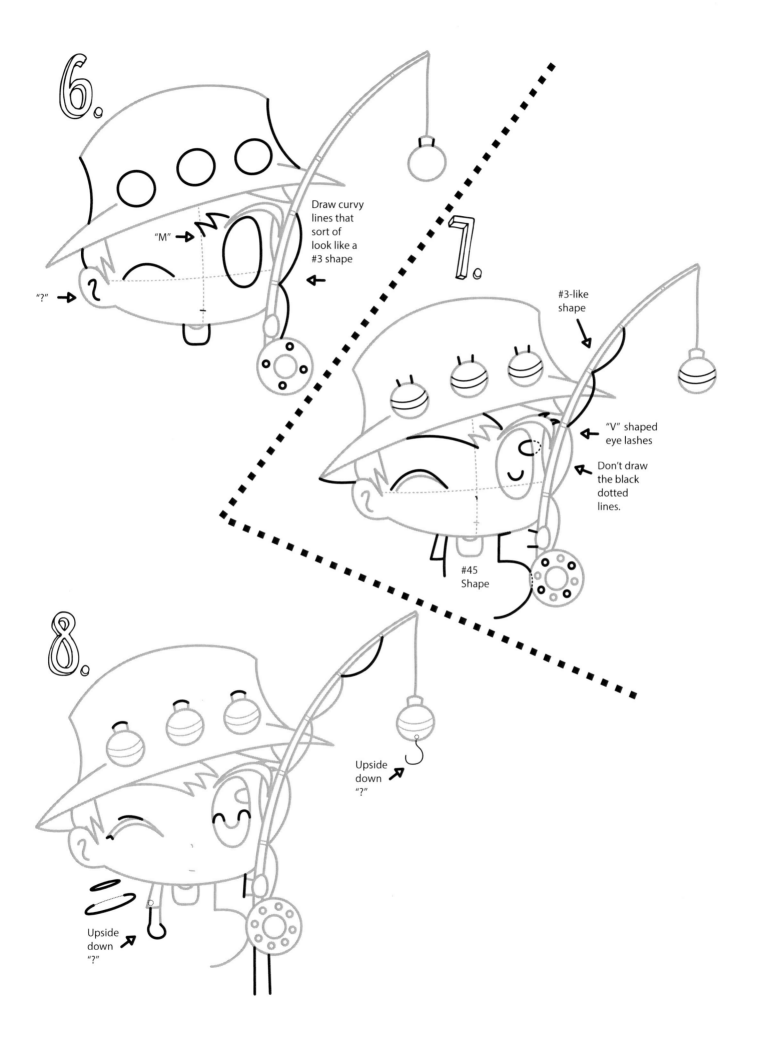

9.

Don't draw the dotted lines.

#7

10.

Draw a bunch of sideways "D"-like shapes.

11.

12.

13.

14.

SILLY PRINCESS

1.

Draw a partial oval. The dotted line part should be drawn lightly as part of it will be erased later on.

2.

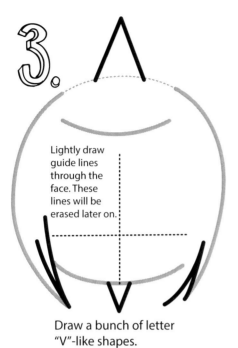

Lightly draw guide lines through the face. These lines will be erased later on.

Draw a bunch of letter "V"-like shapes.

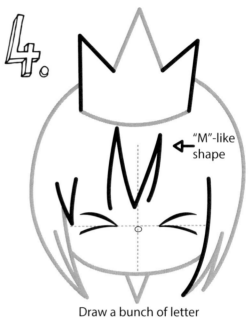

← "M"-like shape

Draw a bunch of letter "V"-like shapes.

← "M"-like shape

← "U"-like shapes

← "m"-like shapes

← "V" + "N" Shapes

← #3 Shapes

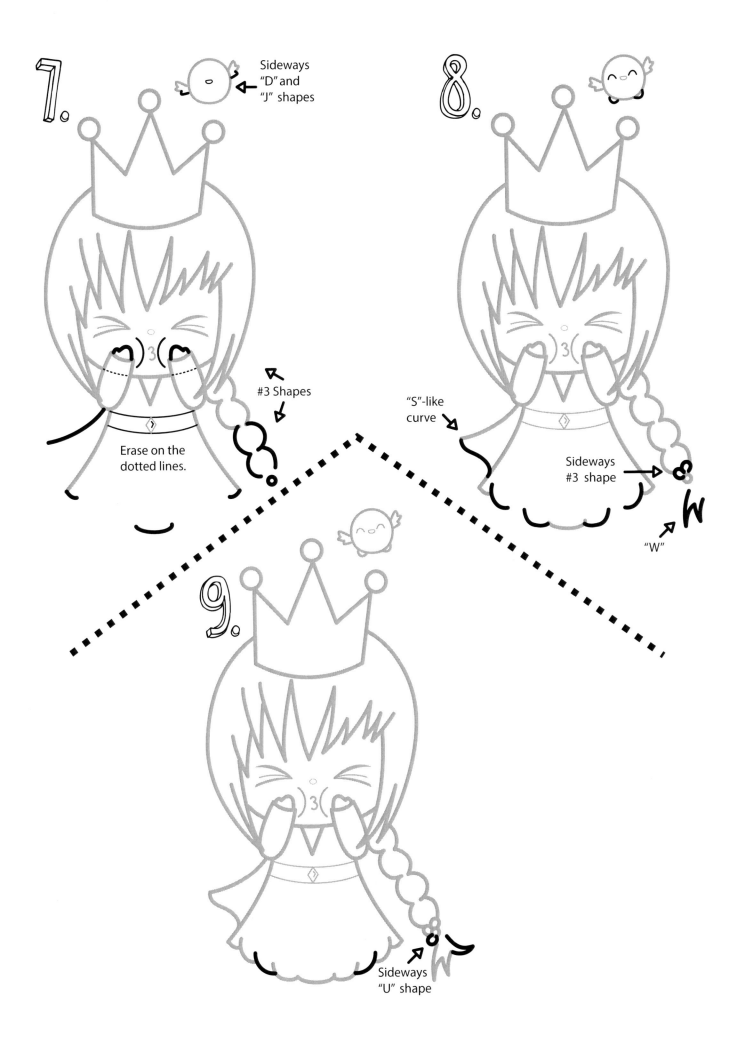

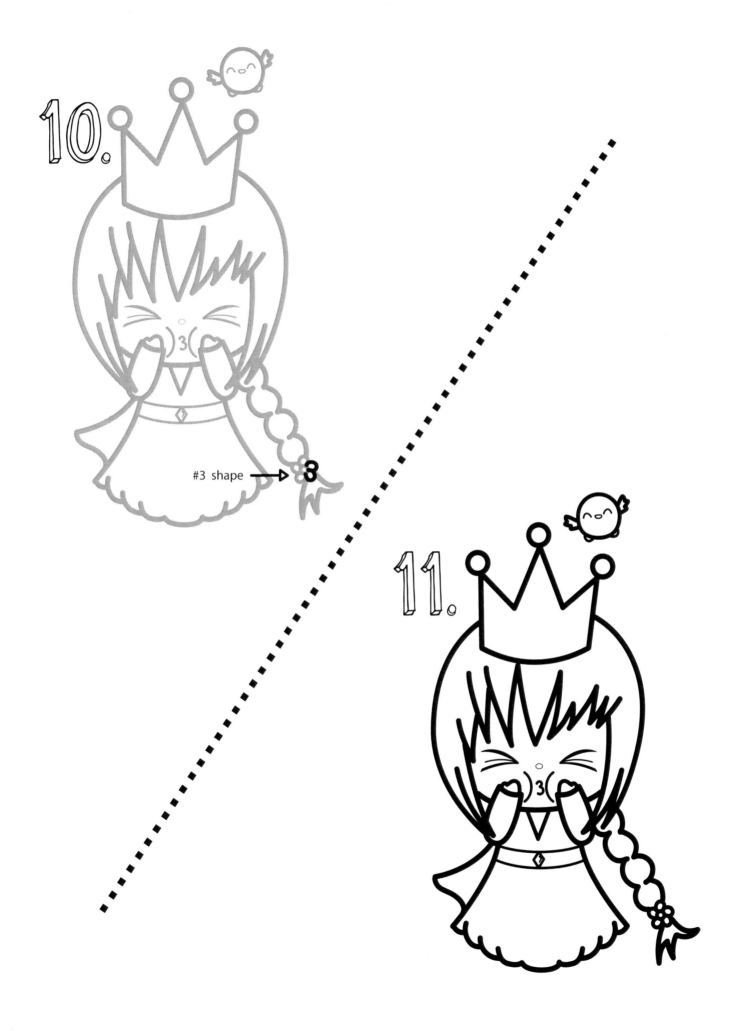

EXCITED ARTIST

1. Lightly draw an oval shaped guide line. Most of this will be erased later on.

2. Lightly draw guide lines through the oval. These lines will be erased later on.

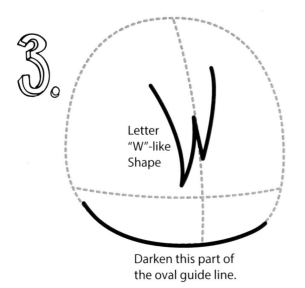
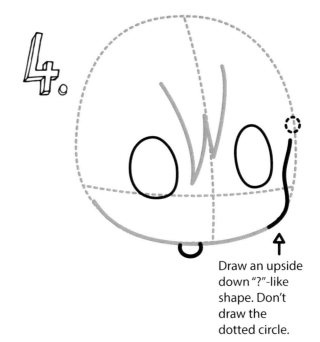

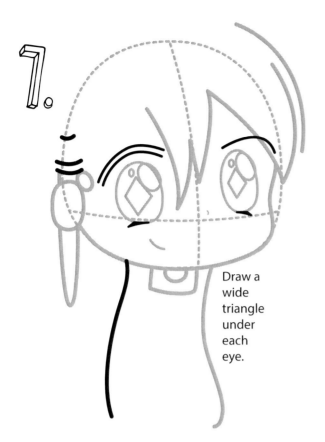

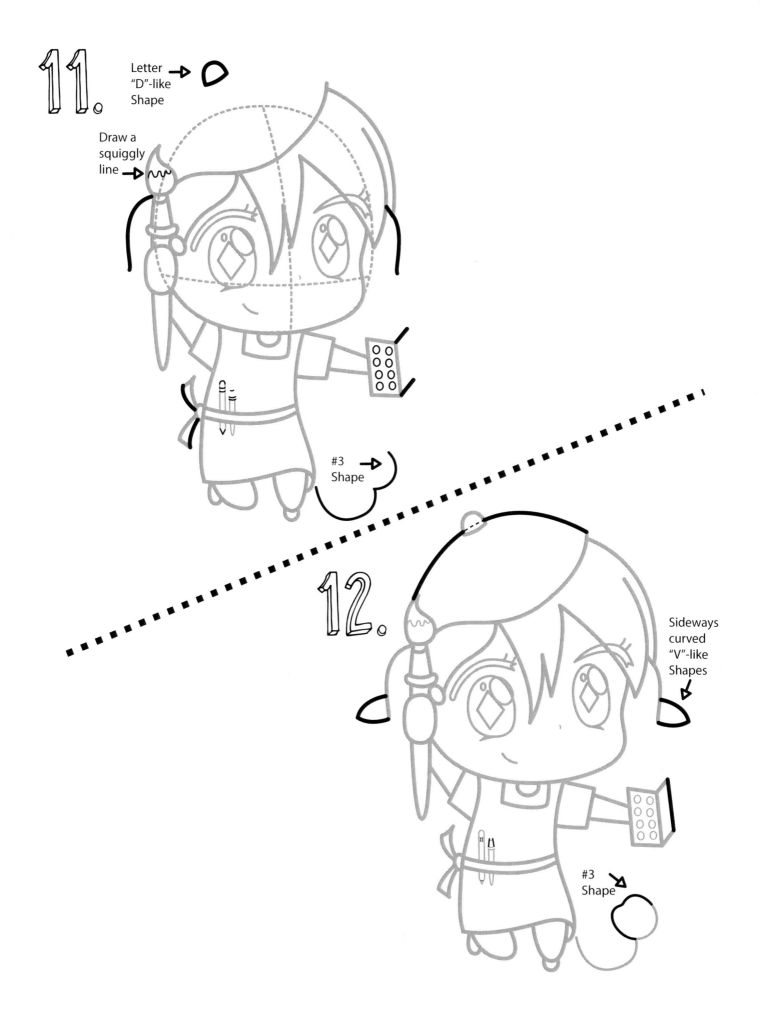

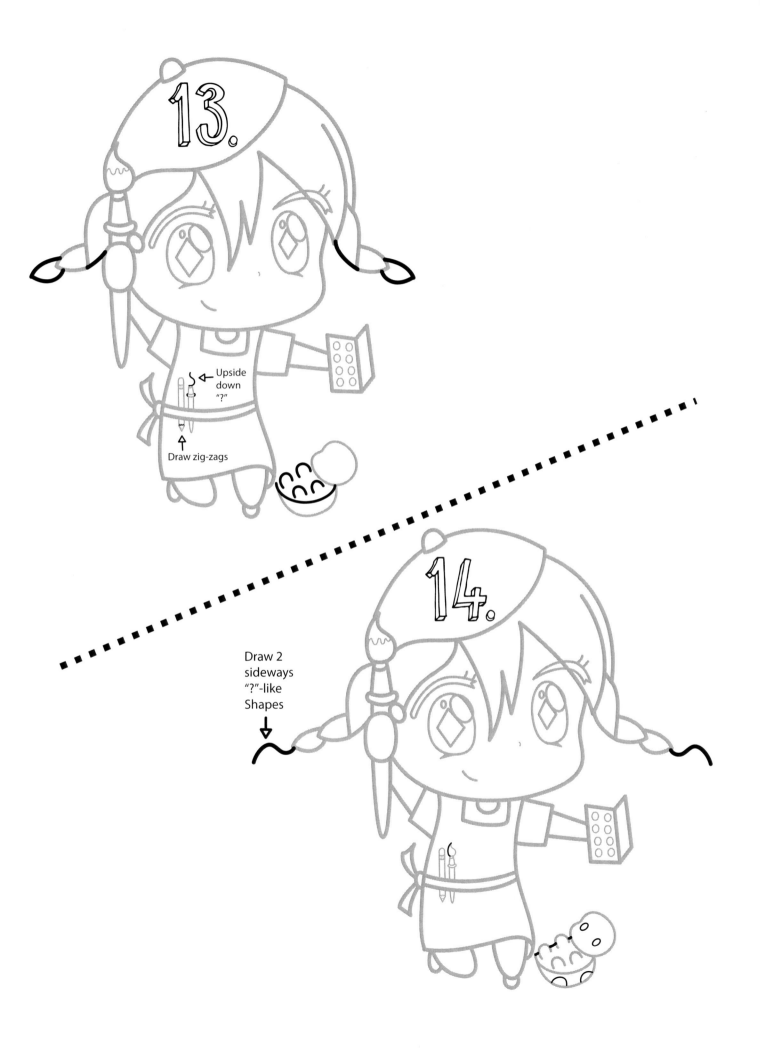

A FEW FREE PAGES FROM MY KAWAII DRAWING BOOKS

KISSING KITTIES

1.

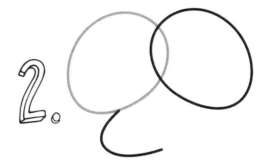

2.

3.
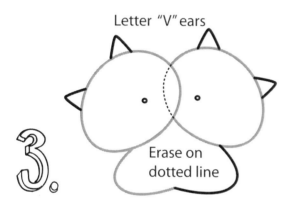
Letter "V" ears
Erase on dotted line

4.
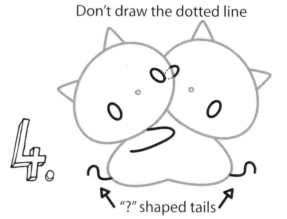
Don't draw the dotted line
"?" shaped tails

5.
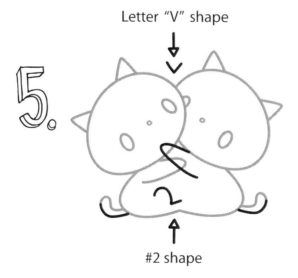
Letter "V" shape
#2 shape

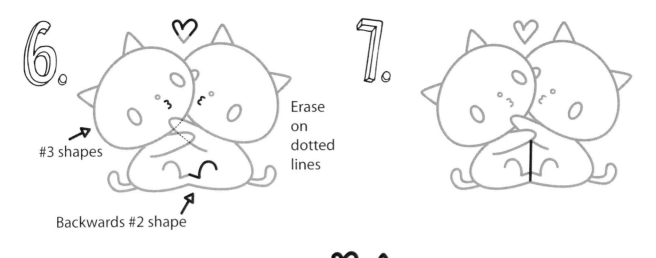

#3 shapes

Erase on dotted lines

Backwards #2 shape

DOG IN SHARK HAT

1.

2.

3. Letter "V" shapes

4. #3 Shape

5. Letter "U" shapes

6.

Erase on dotted lines

A FEW FREE PAGES FROM MY COOL STUFF BOOKS

BOY PUSHING ELEPHANT OFF OF PAPER

Here is another cool paper folding-over project. Draw an elephant on one side of the page and a boy on the other. When you fold it over, you have the boy pushing the elephant.

1. First of all, you need to draw a cartoon boy on the right side of a piece of paper turned on its side. I will show you how to draw him below.

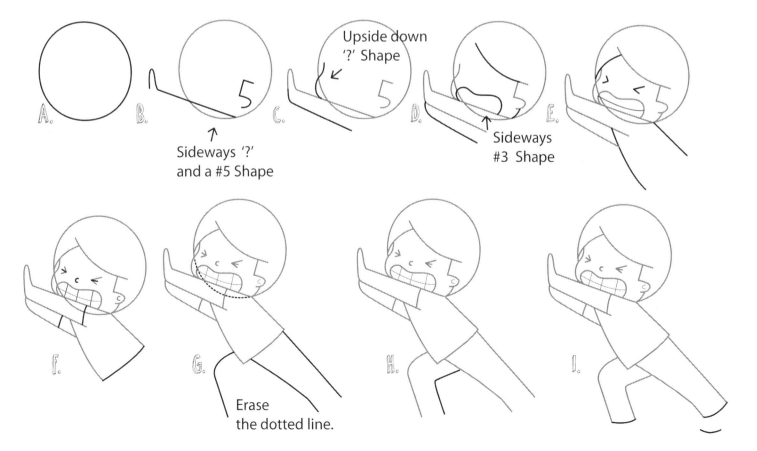

A.

B. Sideways '?' and a #5 Shape

C. Upside down '?' Shape

D. Sideways #3 Shape

E.

F.

G. Erase the dotted line.

H.

I.

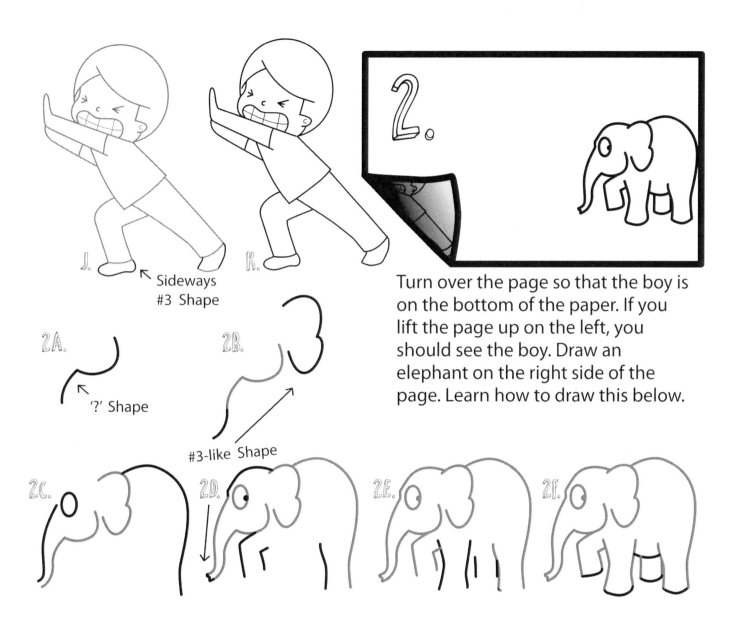

Turn over the page so that the boy is on the bottom of the paper. If you lift the page up on the left, you should see the boy. Draw an elephant on the right side of the page. Learn how to draw this below.

3. Now roll / curve the paper over and match up the boy's hands with the elephant. It will look like the kid is pushing the elephant off of the paper. Really cool!

Box Rising Off of Paper

Here is a cool 3-dimensional effect that is quite simple to draw. It really will look like a cute square is rising off of the paper.

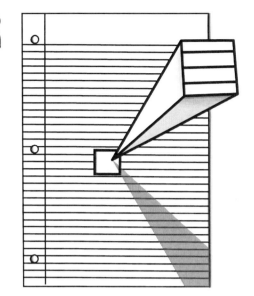

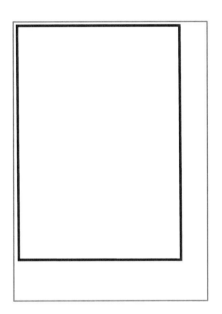

1. Draw a rectangle on the upper left side of a piece of paper.

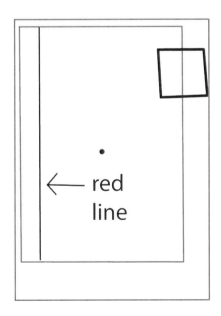

2. Draw a light red line along the left side of the rectangle. Draw slightly slanted rectangle on right side. Draw a dot on the page.

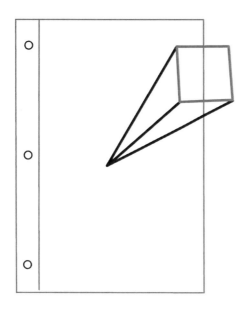

 Draw lines from the rectangle down to the point you drew. Draw 3 circles on left side of page.

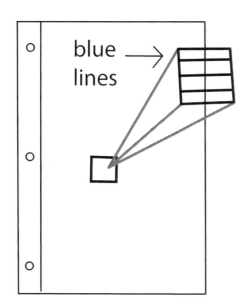

 Draw a smaller rectangle around the point. Draw 3 blue lines on the bigger rectangle.

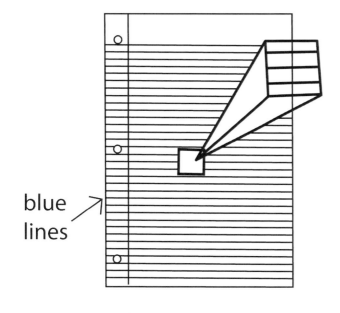

 Draw blue lines around the shapes that you drew.

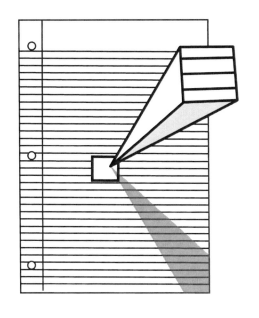

 Draw a gray cast shadow by drawing 2 outward slanted lines that form a triangle. Fill it in gray. You should be able to see the lines thru the shadow. Use a lighter gray to shade the right side of the paper tower.

Shade the left side of the holes + rectangle

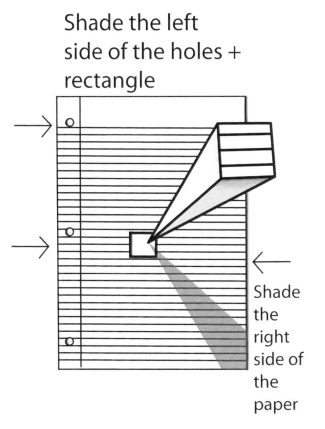

Shade the right side of the paper

 Add some very light shading to the top of the paper tower. Add darker shading to the right side of the piece of paper, as well as the left side of the paper holes and the cut out rectangle.

GUY FALLING OFF YOUR PAPER

This is a cool drawing trick that will amaze your friends. It will actually look like a cartoon boy is hanging off of your paper. Find out how below.

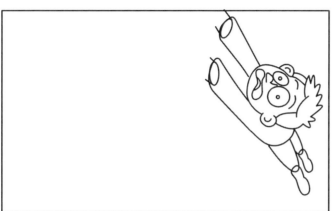

1. First of all, you need to draw a cartoon boy on the right side of a piece of paper turned on its side. We will show you how to draw him below.

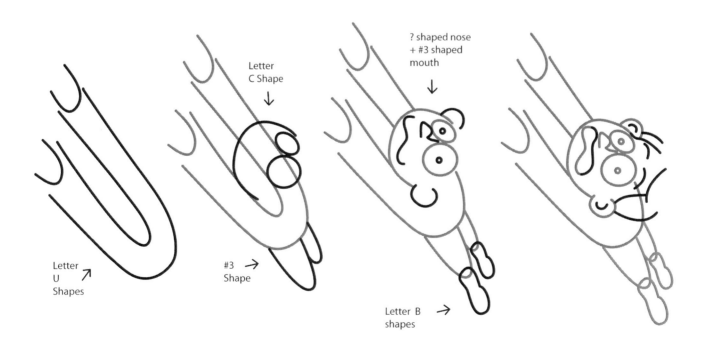

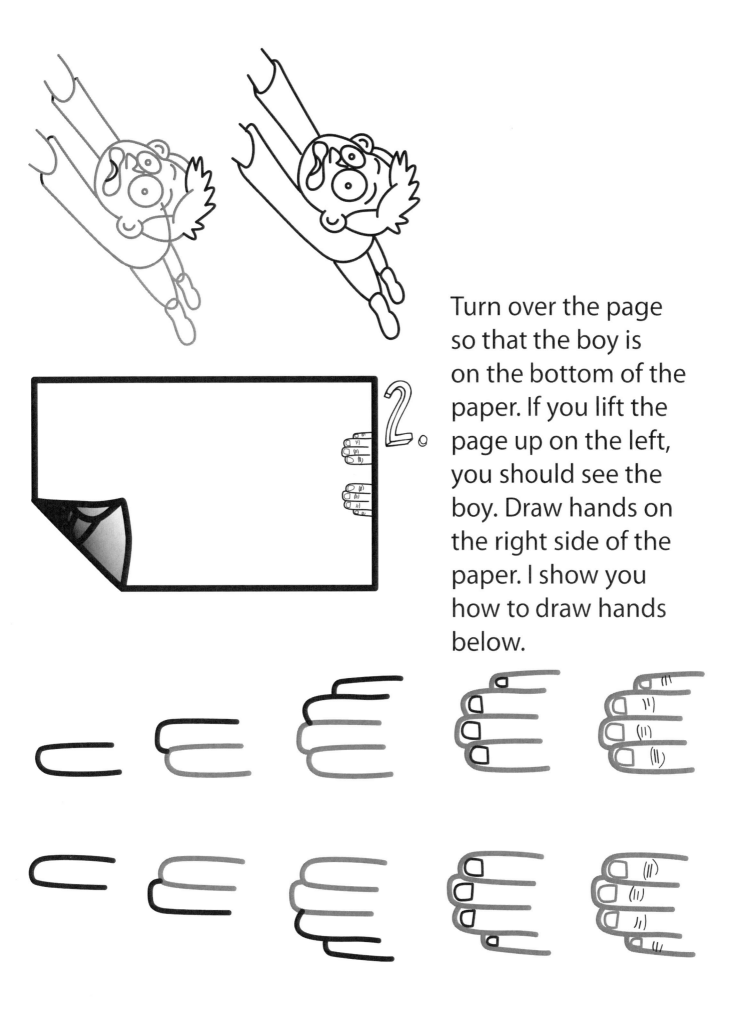

Turn over the page so that the boy is on the bottom of the paper. If you lift the page up on the left, you should see the boy. Draw hands on the right side of the paper. I show you how to draw hands below.

3. Now roll / curve the paper over and match up the hands with the arms. It will look like a 3d person is hanging off of your paper! Cool... isn't it?!!!

A FEW FREE PAGES FROM MY CHIBI BOOK

CUTE PANDAS

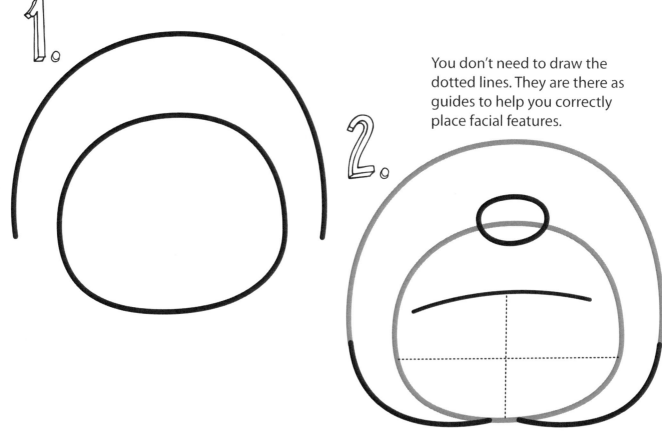

You don't need to draw the dotted lines. They are there as guides to help you correctly place facial features.

Our Other Books

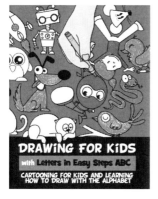

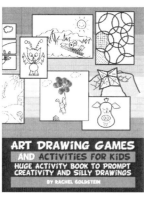

Please Give Us Good Reviews on Amazon! This book is self-published so we need to get the word out! **If You Give us a 5 Star Review**, and Email us About it, We Will Do a Tutorial Per Your Child's Request and Post it On DrawingHowToDraw.com

Made in United States
North Haven, CT
01 December 2021